the SNOWBOUND ANTHOLOGY

A Story of the Blizzard of 1949
and Other Nebraska Stories

the SNOWBOUND ANTHOLOGY

A Story of the Blizzard of 1949
and Other Nebraska Stories

ANDREW STANTON POLLOCK

SNOWBOUND. Copyright © 2019 by Andrew Stanton Pollock. All rights reserved.

ISBN: 978-1-7333926-0-0

Cover Photograph: 703 TIME PASSAGES © 2019 by Michael Forsberg, Lincoln, Nebraska

Cover Design: Redbrush, Lincoln, Nebraska

Published in the United States of America. Goose Creek Press, Goose Creek Book Co., 1448 Pioneers Road, Pleasant Dale, Nebraska 68423.

Dedicated to Jack Pollock, my late father. For me, dad embodied the spirit of western Nebraska perfectly: humble, authentic, looking backwards and forwards without a blink in between.

There are some things you learn best in calm, and some in storm.
~ Willa Cather, The Song of the Lark

CONTENTS

Acknowledgments 1

Introduction 3

Snowbound: A Story of the Blizzard of 1949 5

Juanita Sullens: An Essay on the Art of Changing Faces 49

Janus: Tales of Ants and Snakes and Growing Up in
Rural Keith County 63

Widower: A Poem about Goose Hunting in Garden County 67

MHS Fine Arts Puts on Remarkable Season Finale:
The Story of Hanano Iwatsuki 71

The Music of Tumbleweed Lexicon: An Essay 75

Floating Bodies and Rattlesnakes: An Essay on Camping and
Hiking at Fort Robinson 77

Burning Breezes: The Story of Massacre Canyon 83

Resources and Further Reading 99

Massacre Canyon Playlist 101

About the Author 102

ACKNOWLEDGMENTS

In the spirit of gratitude that comes from a third grader who has not yet grown a chip on his shoulder, thank you, Karen Peters, who taught me to love words in grade school. Thanks also to Dixie Wilson, my English teacher in junior high, and Anita Burge, who taught me how to study good literature at Ogallala High School. Special thanks to editor extraordinaire, Betsy Rowson Zahorjan, for helping me make sense, sound better, and laugh at myself, and to John Janovy, Jr. for critique, guidance, and connecting Betsy and me. And thank you, Julee Hatton, my librarian friend, for your research and encouragement.

My first acknowledgement for independent artistry is a humble thank you to Mike Forsberg for the use of his excellent photograph *703 Time Passages* on the cover of this book. The number relates to Mike's system of organizing his photographs; the remainder of the title relates to the expression you find. It is not the Sullens' house. Theirs was a ranch: one story. Snow has not drifted to the eaves, like it did Wauneta's prison. Those are not human footprints approaching the abandoned farmhouse—the footprints of Robert and the Army bulldozer driver—as I first imagined when I saw the marks in the snow. They are the tracks of three deer. The old farmhouse is in Seward County. To me, the photograph speaks to the beautiful impermanence of life.

For showing me the Blue Water battle site and excellent lessons on history and perspective, thank you Jean Jensen. You are a delightful soul.

To my mother, herself a child of the Sandhills, thank you for telling me the story of Wauneta Sullens, the oatmeal cookies' recipe, and for reading *Tumbleweed Lexicon*. I am pleased my toughest critic enjoyed it!

Deep gratitude to former state Senator Tom Baker of Trenton, Nebraska, for graciously spending half a day showing me around Massacre Canyon and telling me about the battle and other area history.

Much of the color for *Snowbound* came from Nebraska's true Sandhillers, people like Lila Churchill, Delores Colburn, Kyle Arganbright, Cleve Trimble, Steve Moreland, Don Hanna, Linda Downing, Mike Young, Mary Young, Bill Quigley, Sen. Deb Fischer, and the late Lt. Gov. Donald F. McGinley, and others who agree and disagree. Many thanks, to each and all of them.

And thank you, dear reader. I hope I have captured something of the spirit of Nebraska for you.

Andrew Stanton Pollock

INTRODUCTION

Let me ease into this. Nebraska is the theme of this collection of works: short fiction, essays, and one poem. *Snowbound* is the first part of a novel I hope to publish in the future. A few other pieces relate to the true story behind *Snowbound*, which my mother told me when I was a boy. It is the story of Wauneta Sullens, who was snowed in a few dozen miles from town, alone in her small ranch house for five weeks during the Great Blizzard of 1949. *Snowbound* is based on Mrs. Sullens's struggles, but is entirely fiction. It is a tragedy, a sad story, and I hope I have artfully captured its soul.

    The essay entitled *Juanita Sullens* gives the historical account of her plight, as I have learned it, and explains the two spellings of her name. The true story of Mrs. Sullens has haunted me since I was a child. My mother, who was twelve when the blizzard struck and was a neighbor of the Sullens', told me the story when I was a boy.

    All but one of the other pieces are recent works. The oldest is a poem about goose hunting in Garden County first published in *Nebraska Life* in 2004. My dad and I were hunting with Dr. Malone, Tom, the local eye doctor, who told me a metaphor that did not dawn on me until I was a man. Only one other work has previously been published. It is a review I wrote this spring of a fine arts performance by local high school students, including our daughter Katie. The *Milford Times* published it along with photographs someone had taken of the performance. It is a fanciful review about an unscripted story that unfolded before an unexpectant audience on a magical night at the Milford High School auditorium. The final work in the collection, *Burning Breezes,* is a fictionalized account of the gruesome 1873 battle fought in what is now called Massacre Canyon. Most of *the short story,* like most of my novel *Tumbleweed Lexicon,* was written to music.

In these works, you will find glimpses and, perhaps, hear songs of the spirits of Nebraska that have haunted and delighted me: Wauneta Sullens, Crazy Horse, Pawnee agent John Williamson, the blanched grama grasses on the hillsides south of Lake McConaughy, the rugged valley of the North Platte River, its confluence with the Blue Water, a turbulent confluence of cultures—one a pristine, cold-water stream bubbling from ancient waters, the other a muddier, more powerful river—the birds of Crescent Lake, the rattlesnakes of the Panhandle, the solitude of the Sandhills, the parched, echoing canyons of Hitchcock County.

Nebraska's spirits—her shadows and sunrises, her battle cries and hymns, her ghosts and beautiful people, the songs she sings—have inspired these stories. I hope you enjoy them.

SNOWBOUND: A STORY OF THE BLIZZARD OF 1949

New Year's Day began as a day everyone likes to see in winter, but seldom does. The sun shone warmly and much of the snow from the previous storms had melted. Cattle and sheep were grazing winter range and growing fat. That is, they would grow fat if this weather held for the rest of the winter. Sometimes there are winters like that.

Roy V. Alleman, *Blizzard 1949*

January 1, 1949. *Everything is gone. Everything is black. Jagged sounds—strange humming, pipes droning, electricity dragging along edges of silence—cut through the blackness. I am falling into the blackness.*

My dear, she is out there where I cannot see. I hear the echoes of her calling, and we are now dancing together. See, for a moment, everything is just all right with the world and one another, and the skies blur, and you begin to think you can see her.

You see the woman, but you do not know her.

Then, everything changes. Noises come from somewhere, and you turn from the noises because they are electric and angry, like the edges of lightning cutting through the blackness. The pressure of its explosion blows through the air like a woman shrieking after an attack, and nothing is the same.

The man knew he was falling asleep. It had taken several hours. There is said to have been lightning on the first night of the blizzard. Thunder came much later.

One

February 12, 1949. "I don't want to tell you," the young man slurred into the darkness.

You could not see him there, lying on his small cot. You could see little in the darkness.

"I don't want to tell you *goodnight* tonight," the young man said into the silence of his jail cell a second time, as though he was answering someone's question.

No one answered. There were no other inmates. The night deputy had grown somewhat used to the young man, who would talk to himself and sometimes sing.

"You have cast a spell on me," the young man said slowly, but passionately, almost desperately in the language of his body, slurring badly, almost lisping.

Again, no one answered. The young rancher had become used to talking with himself. He had been here several times.

Tonight, he had not seemed as bad, not to the deputy.

* * * * *

When I have been dancing to music at the bar in a state of utter oblivion and denial, if not downright absolution, dancing alone, drunk to the point of the gutter, and someone has to drag me home or to the sheriff's, I am talking to you, dear. I am singing my best to you, dear. I want to come to you.

I want to come be with you, come hell and damnations. I'd cast all my soul into the fire and brimstone and the nothing but tomorrow if I could—

At least I got my scotch.

You have cast a spell on me.

* * * * *

"Jesus, Sullens, shut the hell up." The slow thudding of the deputy's voice came through the darkness like a slowly flashing light. "You're gonna drive me crazy, you batshit-crazy bastard. This little jail ain't institutional enough for you. Quit talking to yourself. You're starting to sing, and you can't sing worth a shit- —especially whatever the hell you's just croaking about. You're messed up, boy."

The young man stood inside the jail cell, behind the bars of the windows on the door. He started laughing at the deputy, whose name always escaped him. He had forgotten what he had been saying, or if he'd been singing. He could not remember, and he would chalk that up to the booze. He needed no convincing. Inebriation has its benefits, but he knew it wasn't a laughing matter, because somewhere his wife was out there, and he knew exactly where, and that was all of the problem.

He had no idea why he had been laughing, and he was angry with himself.

It went something like that. You can never be certain.

* * * * *

"I'm sorry," the young man, Robert, said to the deputy, as though resigned to what seemed the only logical comment, if there was any. He did not, himself, understand.

"It's okay, Robert. I know it's gotta be goddamn hard. I don't know how I'd take it. I know there's no way I can understand. You're gonna see her soon."

The jail was quiet for a few moments before Robert answered.

"I don't mean to complain," Robert Sullens said at last.

"You ain't complaining," the deputy said after a time. "I don't know what the hell you was saying. I quit trying to understand. That's what makes it weird to me. You're talking, and I'm hearing you, and I quit trying to listen. It's like you're speaking Española. I know you're saying something. I just quit trying to understand."

"I'm sorry," said Robert Sullens.

"Hell, don't apologize, Sullens," the deputy said, "but to be honest with you, you are kinda giving me the damn *jeebies*."

"It's nothing but *horsefeathers,* I know—I know, if I remember De-

Beck correctly," the young man named Robert Sullens said because he was drunk.

"No. It's not that," the deputy said, as though he understood. "I know you're making sense enough, even though I quit trying to make sense out of it, or whatever the hell—It's that sometimes it sounds like you're talking to me, but I know you're not. It's just weird, that's all."

"I am truly sorry, Juliette," said the man named Sullens. "I knoweth not what thyself sayeth."

"Shut the hell up," said the deputy. "You were talking to your wife. At least, I hope to hell you were. Go to bed, Sullens. That's a better place than you deserve. I gotta get some sleep."

Sullens chuckled at the man.

* * * * *

In the darkness of his jail cell, the young rancher thought of his wife dancing the way she liked to dance, even on the lawn. He found it funny that she liked to dance by herself, as though she was in love and expressing her love up toward the sky for the sparrows to see. For a simple sparrow—he laughed at himself for thinking of it that way. He found it funny how she danced, but he liked watching her, and he loved her.

"I don't want to tell you goodnight tonight," he said again.

Two

January 1, 1949. Coolness on the breath of easterly winds surprised the young woman. She had not seen ripples lapping that way on the lake near their ranch house before. It was as if the ripples were unsure where they were going. They were not strong waves blowing from the north or the west with assertion. The lake seemed strangely animate.

The young woman thought of her husband.

Wauneta Sullens had long been prone to drama. She imagined herself with dark skin and black hair, not the pale skin and light hair she knew others saw. She was pretty, she knew, and she always wondered why she imagined herself differently. It had always been that way.

"Where are you, darling?" the young woman spoke into the wind.

After there had been time for answer, she spoke again: "Come home. Dance with me."

She began to sway with something you could not see.

The woman saw her bare arms as she swayed and danced. The air had been warm for the first day of the new year. The woman saw her skin was fair. Alone on the dry grass of their lawn and standing with her back to their small ranch house, the woman stretched her neck and joined the sky in a dance only her hands and soul could fathom. She could feel herself *growing colder,* but she let herself settle into the cold, accepting its touch.

"Come home, darling," she sang and repeated into the silence. "Don't be gone long. *You know I can't reach out my hand for nothing.*"

A year before, Robert and Wauneta Sullens had moved into the wooden house and painted it tawny brown with dark brown trim. The house—their first home—was a simple rectangle, nearly a square. It was built by a Kinkaider who filled the house with hope in the early 1900s.

The cleaning of the house kept Wauneta occupied, if not content.

If loneliness in the city, when the windows were closed, was one type of loneliness, then loneliness in the middle of nowhere was an altogether different loneliness. She had learned to milk the cow and enjoyed helping Robert with the chores in the barn by feeding the horse while he cleaned its stall.

Wauneta loved her time with Robert. They talked with one another about their lives and lighthearted things as blithely as any young couple, but she missed talking with women about things she wanted to talk about, and Robert was away all day, out riding fence or checking cattle in the pasture, or doing all the things Wauneta did not want to talk about. She read to keep her mind occupied. She had been reading Faulkner the entire time since they moved into their ranch house in the Sandhills. Wauneta told herself she was Dilsey Gibson. She would endure, occupied by duty.

Wauneta swayed and danced as she took down clothes she had aired in the afternoon sunshine. After placing the corduroy blue work shirt she had given her husband for Christmas in the bushel basket she used for laundry, the young woman began dancing differently. She no longer simply swayed. She stepped gracefully, easily. Wauneta did not pretend to be dancing with her husband. It was not that. She danced with subtle grace and, at times, the grandness of a ballerina, as though a symphony was playing an adagio *once more for the ages* behind her.

Wauneta closed her eyes, giving off the appearance of a dream. She thrust her chin softly but with expression toward the earth's four corners and all around. Her head bowed as she moved it in oddly suggestive ways. Wauneta took small steps, then large, smooth strides. She danced softly, but did not dance on her toes.

Her arms swung as though listening to her hands. They stretched to clouds scattered across the sky and came together as though folded in prayer. Wauneta danced until light mist began to spin around her on a north wind.

A sparrow on the clothesline pole appeared to watch the young woman. The bird ruffled its feathers and cocked its head as though wondering if she was longing for her lover.

Before snow dusted the young woman's freckled nose, she looked out across the hills northeast toward Valentine, the town where her husband was going. She looked over the fences the homesteader had strung long ago to surround his crops. The first ranchers had left the fences to keep cattle out of their yard and the building where her husband now kept his new John Deere *Model M*.

The tractor with a green chassis and yellow wheels was Robert Sullens's first acquisition after selling the first hundred head of Herefords he had raised. The barbed-wire fences kept the cattle out of the chicken coops, the barn where they kept their horses and milk cow, and a few other sheds.

Her husband had painted all of the outbuildings the same color as the house the summer before: a tannish brown color on the walls, and a darker, reddish brown on the corners and trim.

Beyond the fences, the young woman looked across the hills of sand; the great, ancient dunes were no longer shifting with the winds. Bluestem, buffalo grass, grama, Indiangrass, and others had taken hold eons ago and had frozen the Sandhills in time. Where the homesteader failed to tame the wild lands with modern implements, the rancher succeeded simply by letting his cattle graze, like the buffalo before them.

Great dunes rose to meet the gaze of the young woman and melted indecipherably into the fading horizon, dunes covered with grasses, dancefloors for the winds. Closer to their ranch house, within the homesteader's fences, but beyond the buildings, the grasses rippled in array, still glowing deeply in their autumn colors with the evening sunlight.

The young woman could not help taking in the grandeur of the sky—the sky in her various hues, slowly shedding them for darkness.

She watched the colors fade as darkness came. She whispered the words of a song she had heard on their Philco radio and remembered.

Once, I thought of skies as blue.
I thought of sky as blue when
I thought of her without clouds
Or colors on edges of day. Now,
I think of sky as dark. But she
Is not yet dark, not this evening-time.

Darkness came over the wild, old lands, the dunes of sands and grasses, and winds, full of songs and emotions. A cold mist frosted Wauneta's blonde hair, and then a drop fell from her hair and touched her freckled nose.

The cold droplet of water drew down the opening of the young woman's blouse.

Today. Wauneta Schneider had studied Greek mythology in college for reasons her father eventually came to understand before he followed her mother to the grave. Her mother died not long after Wauneta's birth.

An only child with an air of otherness that did not seem superior or proud, Wauneta was exquisitely smart. Being intellectual came naturally to her. It was not a spirit she sought or even contemplated. She wore her spirits without giving an air of haughtiness or anything resembling pride. She seemed content, like everything around her pleased her in a way that passed understanding.

Dancing came naturally to Wauneta Schneider, and she loved to go to the dances, and dance with other girls and boys, and when she came home, it was then her father believed she was somewhere else. At some point—he was never quite certain when—the young widower found he could not understand his daughter.

Wauneta studied mythology and danced. She wanted to go on to get a master's degree in fine arts, and her father told her that was acceptable, *so long as she married rich*. She laughed with her father when he teased her that way. Wauneta loved her father, and Heinrich Schneider loved his daughter, but he did not like her dancing. He said he always thought it led to dark places.

The Schneiders lived in Omaha. Wauneta's father had become *filthy rich*, as he would say in reflection, selling commercial real estate, but lost most of what he had in the thirties and never recovered. Heinrich Schneider held on to some properties, paid for his daughter's education, and died before he had to worry about more. It was only in the moment of giving up his ghost that Heinrich Schneider understood his daughter's spirit.

Three

January 1, 1949. Robert Sullens had driven his pickup into town for supplies and groceries. The young man's dark brown hair was cut so closely to the scalp that his hair looked lighter than it was. His eyes were charcoal gray, almost smoky, and he remained wiry and tough from his days wrestling in the 114-pound class at the University.

March 21, 1947. Robert Sullens came from the Sandhills. His father had been an optometrist in Valentine. Robert wanted to become a rancher, and he'd learned how to ranch on the largest operation north of the Pecos. He knew he would be a great rancher and would one day own one hundred thousand acres like his boss, whom he admired like a father.

Robert first met Wauneta at the university in Lincoln. They met on campus where a band from Kansas City was covering music some Texan named Goree Carter had written. The Student Culture Club had brought the group in as part of the festivities to celebrate the first day of spring.

There were a few college kids dancing, mostly girls, when Robert walked into the study lounge called the Crib at the Student Union. A large guy who looked like he had never met an enemy, or at least anyone brave or stupid enough to challenge him, was playing the saxophone. A crazy-looking cat with bloodshot eyes and hair cut so close it looked like it was glued to his scalp was playing the drums. A man in a tuxedo was playing the grand piano, which was an often-used piece of the Crib. The smartly dressed guy playing guitar sang. Their music was remarkably good. Robert had never heard anything like it.

The young man stood and listened to the band, as though he was mesmerized. He stood and watched the other college students dancing, and he did not recognize any of them, but a fair-skinned girl with the lightest blonde hair and most distinct features—the bold curve of her eyebrows; her slight, turned-up nose; her full, dark lips; her sharp cheekbones; the freckles on her cheeks—made him laugh to himself that she must be *elfin*. The distinct features of her face fit with her elfin hair. She looked up from her dancing and caught the young man's eye. She stared into his eyes for longer than a moment and kept dancing as she looked at the young man in the cowboy hat.

It was as though the young lady with the fair skin, blonde hair, and blue eyes, as well as one of the other girls, understood the music in their dance. And as they danced, it was as though for something more fleet than a moment. The young woman was asking the young man if he wanted to dance with her. He smiled, then turned and laughed when a friend of his told him to quit gawking at the pretty girls.

"Who's that one?" the young man asked.

"That one is Wauneta something," the young man's friend said, looking toward the girl. "I don't know what the hell her last name is. Listen to that guitar, Sullens. We're here for this music, not the girls."

To Robert Sullens, it seemed as though something was wrong. The jazz was upbeat. While jazz was not something he heard all the time, he'd heard good jazz before. The strange part was the guitar. The guitar did not sound like jazz guitar. The sound from the guitar was something Robert Sullens believed his father would not like, if his father had still been around.

Robert's father had died of a heart attack the first winter the young man was at the university. Driving back home from somewhere, Robert's father had driven off the road. The car took out Maurice Simmons's barbed wire fence and came to rest in his pasture. The body of Arthur Bruce Sullens was frozen when they found him.

Robert Sullens's mother died during childbirth.

Robert was their only child.

After listening to the music for much longer than a moment and letting his mind wander, Robert conceded in the quiet of his own mind that he liked the guitar, especially when he saw the young woman named Wauneta dancing to it.

Abruptly, he fell for the young woman.

* * * * *

It took a Robert a couple trips to his pickup, where he and his roommate Reuben had stashed a quart of scotch, before he finally danced with her.

"That's some kinda dancing, cowboy," the girl said to young man with the large hat.

"How'd you know I was a cowboy?"

"I smelled the scotch."

"You don't like my dancing."

"You dance like you've had too much scotch, but that's okay. At least you're dancing."

"You don't like my belt buckle."

The young woman chuckled. "What on earth are you talking about? "If you don't know, I'd like to get to know you better."

"I like your belt buckle. If you wish to know the truth, that's how I knew you were a cowboy."

The young man laughed at himself. His friend Reuben, watching from the other side of the bar, was laughing, too, not knowing the reason he was laughing, and not caring for a moment.

The young woman and the young man danced with one another, and looked into one another's eyes. The band was playing a slow song that dallied along like an old man musing fondly over the ebony and ivory keyboard of the grand piano. Suddenly, abruptly, the singer broke in. "Hey, ya'll. Bugeaters, Cornhuskers, Cornbuggers—what they calling you these days? Bugeared Platypus, I be hearing on the streets of the city, Bugeared Platypus," the man sang, and his band was laughing so hard you'd wonder how they kept playing. The piano player in the black tuxedo with the white shirt and black tie rocked back and forth, laughing as he played.

"Take me downtown for some ice cream," the young woman said to the young man.

"I would like that," the man responded.

They walked out of the Union. "Look at the stars," said the young woman.

"Not nearly as good as where I come from," the young man said.

"Where do you come from?" she asked.

"My name is Robert Sullens," he said, not answering her question. "You are Wauneta."

"How did you know?"

"My friend told me."

"Nice you meet you, Robert."

"Let's walk and get some ice cream."

"You don't mind walking?" she asked.

15

"Not at all. Do you want to get your friends?"

"No," the young lady said and started walking, and the young man took a large step to catch up to her.

"Do you like that music?" she asked after he had softened into her pace a few steps later. The young man had not spoken again.

"I guess we're going to get ice cream," he said.

The young woman laughed. "Do you like the music?" she asked again.

"I loved the music, but I don't think I'm supposed to."

"Your momma wouldn't approve?" the young woman teased him.

"Not if she was still around to hear it."

"I'm sorry, she said. I lost both my Mom and my Daddy."

"Me too."

They learned they were only children. Love is as simple as it is sublime. There really wasn't one thing either of them questioned about the other, including their appearances, other than the fact that he was going back to the Sandhills to take over his family's ranch, probably a year before he graduated. He'd finish the semester, but would not come back to the University after summer.

They had not walked far, and the doors to the Student Union remained open behind them. Students milled outside the doors and on the plantation-style balcony of the Union, smoking and laughing. The evening was unusually warm. The man and woman could hear the music drifting through the open doors.

"I love this song," Wauneta said, stopping. She stopped, stood there, and then started dancing in a way the young man had never seen a person dance. The young woman approached him and started dancing closely to him, and he put his hands upon her waist, and she drew him closer with her arms around his neck, and he nudged her chin with his, and they kissed.

The band moved into another slow blues song. The man and woman looked into one another's eyes. His were charcoal gray. Hers were blue. They were alone. The few students milling outside the doors paid them no attention.

Four

Today. They fell in love. They married in her parents' church. They honeymooned on Punta Mita and fell more deeply in love. In the few months before they married, Wauneta wondered why she had not just married Robert and called it a day. She enjoyed the planning. She enjoyed the details. She enjoyed the time with her bridesmaids, the showers friends of her parents threw, and the party Robert's best man Isaac threw for the prospective couple in Valentine.

She did not like living alone. Between graduation and their wedding, Wauneta lived in her parents' home in Omaha. She had sold it. She would move out not long before their New Year's Eve wedding. She did not know what it was about being alone that had begun to bother her. Everything worried her. Would someone try to come into the house, break a window, or be standing in a corner she had forgotten to check? Or perhaps something would happen, and she would not know what to do. The electricity would quit working, and she would have to call for help. Sometimes, she knew, she worried about silly things, but they did not seem silly while she was worrying.

Wauneta graduated with her degree in Greek mythology not long after her father died. She settled his estate with no trouble and moved into his house in May. Wauneta worked at the library at Creighton University and began planning for the wedding.

She enjoyed the house in the summertime. At first, she did not mind being alone. It was cooler in the house than outside, much cooler, and she kept the windows open at night. The screens kept out the bugs.

One evening, Wauneta fell asleep in her father's old study. It was a small room with a large picture window. Smaller windows on either side were open. She had been sitting in her father's recliner, reading. The lamp was on.

In the night, after sleeping for perhaps an hour—she did not know—Wauneta was awakened by the loud humming of insects. Insects, moths, mayflies, and bugs she had never imagined before clung to the window, as though they were trying to reach her.

After that, Wauneta kept the windows closed at night, but she did not like to keep them closed. She liked the winds blowing air through her house, but she could no longer tolerate the sound of the insects. After the insects had died in the fall, she opened the windows again, but then winter came, and it became too cold.

Five

January 1, 1949. Robert's gray felt cowboy hat sat beside him while he was driving, and his coat was on the passenger end of the bench seat of his pickup. The first nineteen miles of the trip to town were on a sand trail road that connected the ranches in the hills. There are no prescribed rules of law or thumb as to the location of a particular ranch house: how far off the highway, how far from your neighbor's house, how far from the nearest property line that had been etched across the grasses in barbed wire.

The remaining twenty-six miles were on a more traveled sand road that served as the highway into Valentine. The last few miles into Valentine, Robert's pickup toughed through snowdrifts as wide as several feet. It was slow going. He arrived much later than he had planned.

* * * * *

In the small kitchen of their ranch house, Wauneta listened over the party line to neighbors talking about the weather. It was acceptable to listen in, or "rubber," as they called it back then, when folks were talking about the weather. Weather was important to the entire community. It was okay to listen to others talking about the weather, but some rubbered after the weather had been discussed.

* * * * *

Pauline Thurston said her husband heard on KOA that "cowboys was supposed to pull their hats down low and brace for high winds today." Her boys had "missed getting home for Christmas, on account of the storm the day before Christmas Eve," and she was worried about more snow.

Someone—Pauline did not recognize the man's voice—said it "was sunny outside before that east wind kicked in before the sun went down."

She heard Joy Fairhead say he felt "like there was a bad storm coming."

* * * * *

Snow blew in that evening. The blizzard hit with an intensity few expected.

It had been less than two months since twenty inches of snow—twenty inches—and a few days of wind had beaten up the Sullens and trapped them at their ranch for a week. That was late November. Around Christmas, snow blew in again and drifted along the fencerows and buildings. Another storm was supposed to be coming, but by now, everyone was getting used to storms.

Robert had heard snow was coming again. It was New Year's Day. He drove his truck to town to get supplies and groceries. Wauneta had told him she'd never be snowed in for an entire week again without enough to eat. She said it might drive her crazy to be snowed in, just the two of them, again. They laughed about it, but something in the way his wife moved or spoke to him made Robert uneasy. He sped along as quickly as he could until the drifts slowed him down. He inched his way into town. He knew he had to get what he needed and head back home.

* * * * *

By the time light had faded from the sky thick with snow, Wauneta's husband had not come home. During the night, winds, confused by the edges of their ranch house, left snow drifted up to the tops of the windows. There was no longer color. Nothing was brown. Nothing was green. Nothing was white. Everything was black outside the house, except in the pale amber glow of the porchlight, where snow angled by in a blur. Darkness loomed behind the meager light. During the night, the wind shifted to the north, and the cold came.

Wauneta kept the porchlight on. It illuminated the yard when heavy snow began to fall in the first hours. The snow early in the night reminded her of snows when she was young and she lived with her mother and father, and flakes of snow drifted slowly to the ground from the light of the city. She smiled as she watched snow falling. Her husband would be home soon. The snow, she thought, was starting to let up.

* * * * *

Earlier in the afternoon, only a few dozen miles northeast, winds whistled another song, strong in the discord and dissonance we think of little and ponder less. They make us uncomfortable. Sometimes we shiver when music haunts us. Granular snow spun sideways below the hidden skies. The wind you could not look into, or your eyes would water. You could not see.

* * * * *

Snow had blown in heavily, drifting across the roads like dunes by the time the young rancher made it to Valentine. He stopped at Hans's U & I grocery store and the Red & White hardware store for some caulking for the windows and door he'd noticed were leaking cold air. Robert tried to drive home after filling up with gas and buying a cup of coffee, but the sheriff's deputy would not let him leave town. Mrs. Briggs at the grocery store told him he was *a fool to have made the trip in the first place*. The young rancher would not make it home that night. Robert Sullens called Wauneta on the telephone at the front desk of the Marian Hotel, where he would spend the night.

* * * * *

"Don't be gone a week, now," she said to him lightly, yet with a trace of tension in the cords of her voice. "I don't know if I could handle being out here all alone."

"I'll be back tomorrow, dear," Robert said. "You have plenty of food and wood, and the lights are on."

"What if I get snowed in?" Wauneta asked, then paused before she went on. "November haunts me," she said, her tone changing and her voice giving a little. Or perhaps it was only the static on the party line.

"I don't like to be alone," she said after a time.

"Wauneta," he said, smiling toward the window. "Storms like November don't come around every year."

"It's a new one," Wauneta said abruptly.

Robert chuckled softly for a moment but broke off. He looked at the woman who was smiling at him from the front desk of the hotel. She chuckled with him. "It'll be all right, Wauneta," he said. "Storms like that don't come along more than every fifty years or so. Dear, last time we had a storm like that here in the Sandhills was back in 1913, if not way back in '91. I told you that."

"I can't help thinking, Robert."

"Can't help thinking what?"

"Can't help thinking what would happen if you never came back, darling."

"Don't go talking that way," her husband admonished lightly. "Tomorrow's a new day. I'll see you then. That I can assure you."

They carried on only a few moments longer. It was not good form to talk long on the party line.

Six

January 2, 1949. Late Sunday morning, Robert called his wife again from the telephone in the Marian. Wauneta stood at the wood table in the kitchen of their ranch house. The light was on and the stove was burning, but it seemed dark. Wauneta told him she had not slept.

"Come home now, Robert," she went on, "and we will keep each other warm underneath the covers."

"Wauneta," the young rancher said, startled.

"Yes?" she asked, then said nothing.

"Dear," he said. "We're on a party line."

"I'm sorry," she said. "What did I say?"

The young man looked at the wall behind the front desk, past the morning clerk, an older man who was looking idly at some records. Robert turned and looked out the windows of the doors of the hotel. Snows blew past in a strange, nameless, and inscrutable mass. The wind blew as if it had lost its mind. The wind had come and declared a new kingdom that would never again permit its inmates laughter, peace, or the warm breath of spring.

"Are you warm enough, dear?" the young man asked his wife.

"Yes, darling, but it feels cold outside. It's like I can feel it out there, even though I am inside. I have a good fire going, Robert. The lights made it seem warmer last night."

"Wauneta," the young man said soberly.

"Yes, Robert. What is it?"

"I cannot make it today, dear," he said stoically.

It was quiet for some time before the man could hear the young woman begin to cry.

They heard a click. Someone had been on the party line.

Robert Sullens was unable to calm his wife. She cried harder. The two of them were alone in the darkness where sounds pierce like light. He heard only her crying. She heard him telling her he was *sorry* and heard the other idle remarks he made with hope in a voice that seemed to give a little—or perhaps it was only the static on the party line.

After what seemed to Robert like a time that would never end, Wauneta hung up the telephone.

Seven

January 4, 1949. By the middle of the first week of the new year, the telephone lines were down. The entire county—all 6,000 understated square miles of county, and most of the Sandhills, most of Nebraska, and much of more than a dozen states—lay under a thick blanket of snow.

Snow blew with winds that roared without relent the first three days. Snow filled the valleys, coated the hills, and consumed the roads like the dunes of sand that had formed the hills eons ago. Roads and railroad lines were closed, and cattle were stranded and starving, isolated for weeks. The snow drifted relentlessly around the Sullens' place. Snow drifted above the windows by the door and all around the house, reaching to the eaves by the time the snow stopped falling from the sky. A drift nearly engulfed their ranch house.

Robert Sullens remained in town. There was no means to reach his wife. Snowplows inched through town and onto roads on the edges of town. There was no way for an airplane to land, and they refused to drop Sullens or let him walk from town or ride a horse to its death.

January 6, 1949. *The Valentine Republican's* local news editor reported that the *newly elected Senator and Mrs. Don E. Hanna Sr. left before the storm hit Saturday for Lincoln where they will make their home at the Hotel Lindell while the Unicameral is in session.*

Concern was felt for several persons and families who were caught in the storm or ventured out after it struck. This morning turned out bright, clear, and still, but the winds of the first three days of the year have piled the snow that fell, plus what was left from the previous storm on Dec. 23 and 24, into drifts up to fifteen feet high in town. City streets and sidewalks are being cleared rapidly and there is no doubt that railroad and highway crews are clearing those arteries. But when rail or highway traffic will be restored remains problematic.

* * * * *

Before snow had piled over their ranch house, snows went whistling past, blurring Wauneta's view. Looking outside, she could not make out a thing. The young woman looked out the window and thought she saw a man standing outside in the snowstorm.

    But it was not a man, standing. Rather, the man was dancing. He danced slowly, but not as though he was holding someone; he swayed slowly to music. It struck her that the young man danced as though he was *giving up the ghost,* although the woman could not understand why those words struck her. She did not stop to understand.

    Snow rushed past the porchlight glow in horizontal lines. The symmetry of lines also struck the young woman—lines the snow etched on the horizon.

    The man faced into the snow, blurring along the blackness. The light shone on the profile of the man, and she did not recognize him.

    Wauneta walked through the window and toward the dancing man.

    The man turned and looked at her without expression.

    At first, she was uncertain, but then she realized who it was. The woman relaxed. She breathed easily, slowly, in rhythm with her movements, which were driven by the movements of the man. She swayed gently as he danced. Her eyes came to accept the darkness—not to accept the darkness, but what she found there. The young man did not take her in his arms, but approached her so closely that she could feel him brush lightly upon her as he danced.

    She then could hear music. She heard it as though the music had begun suddenly, far away, in the midst of a song—a simple dirge she had not heard before.

    The music struck her, and the woman began to dance slowly in the darkness with the man. She swayed with the man as though the music were driving them in timeless and mysterious ways. Together they danced as music played and night grew older. Snow rushed upon her back in wind's reckless osculations, danced up the curve of her neck, and tousled her hair.

    The woman looked into the eyes of the man.

* * * * *

The pretty blonde-haired woman was dreaming. Wauneta Sullens was walking in her sleep. She stood, staring into the window and her dim reflection. Snow covered the picture window. She could not see a speck of sky.

The woman was not standing. She was dancing. Although she understood no words, she swayed slowly with the songs of winds. She had been comfortable, dancing with the man, but suddenly she grew cold, and she drew the man to her.

The man became lost in the way she danced with the music that was moving him, and he took the woman in his arms.

She felt the strength of his arms and chest, and drew him closer.

Eight

January 13, 1949. *The new year brought one of Nebraska's famous blizzards,* reported the Simeon correspondent for the *Republican. It will rank along with those of January 12, 1888, February 9, 1891, and March 14, 1913. Old-timers are of different opinions as to the relative severity of the storm.*

After ten days of near isolation, conditions in town are rapidly returning to normal, although many huge snowdrifts will remain until spring to remind us of one of the worst storms in years, the editor wrote from the comfort of his office in Valentine. Robert's hands trembled as he drank his coffee. *Highway 83 was still closed both north and south of Valentine. The Valentine Air Service has been busy from dawn until dark daily, delivering food and supplies to snowbound ranches, flying ranchers over their holdings in search of cattle, and locating stranded persons. R. E. Brickley and Ansel Wrage suffered severe, but as yet undetermined, losses.*

* * * * *

"Robert, I will lock you up if you try to walk to your ranch," the sheriff said to him after the young man was found in the hills the second time. He only got a half mile the second time. The first time, they caught him on a trail road ten miles from town. They had to chase him down, but it was not terribly difficult. He was slowed by the snow drifts. They took him to the county jail. The young man was sweating, and the deputies had to hold him back. He was lunging for the door.

They held him back until he relaxed his arms, and they slowly let him go.

"Can I just stay here tonight, Albert?" asked the young rancher.

"Tonight's all right, Robert," said the sheriff. "You just gotta stay outta that scotch. Shit, man. You know you can't do that to yourself. It makes you stupid, son. We're gonna get you to her. You know that, Robert. I promise. You've known me a long time."

"I've known you two years, and there's very little between us other than the forty miles of highway and seventeen of sand."

One of the deputies laughed, but the sheriff knew the young man was serious, even as he slurred. He slurred his words to a heavy lisp. He had lisped as a child, and they had thought him "retarded" until he was in junior high. He got a scholarship to attend the university where he met Wauneta.

He did well, but a bright mind and good education shiver and don't shine much, lying on a cot in a cold, dark cell of the jail of Cherry County. The county seat was nearly sixty miles from the young man's ranch house.

Late in the night, the man awoke, standing in his cell. His hands were gripping the bars on his door. He could see the light of the moon on the glass of the window on the wall of the jailhouse. He held the bars and looked into the darkness beyond.

"What are you thinking? I can't fathom what you are thinking. I am locked in this cell in the county jail, and I cannot imagine what you are thinking. I'm sorry," the young man said to the darkness. His words fell short of the window.

* * * * *

She tried to climb out of the house, to crack the windows on their hinges or break them. She needed to tend to the animals in the barn. They had not been fed for a week.

She broke several windows, the last one with her hand. She was pressing on the window to see how hard she could press. She was not strong, so she leaned her weight into the window, but she weighed little by that time. She pushed with her legs, which rested on the wooden floor, and anchored her feet against the weight of the table behind her.

The legs of the table were strong, thick cuts of cottonwood. The young rancher had made the table himself a year before they had married, while he was living on the ranch alone. The tabletop was also made of heavy cottonwood from the center of an old, dying tree. She pushed hard on the glass, and it broke and cut her hand.

Snow melted in through the window not long after she had broken it. Water dripped upon the windowsill where she had rested her head after she started to see light through the snow on the outside of the window. Long after the wind had ceased to howl and long after the last drift had mounted against the windows, she saw light through the bottom of the window. To her, it looked like morning. She remembered hunting for Easter eggs on her grandfather's patio, where sun drifted in.

The sun was shining outside and glistened on drops of water falling from the eaves.

* * * * *

Robert stood, looking out beyond the cell window. His hands felt cold on the bars.

He told her goodnight, but he knew she was not listening. She may have told him goodnight, but she meant something else he would never understand. He pretended that he did not care to understand. He looked out the window, but only moonlight touched the edges of the windows and made them shimmer. Nothing more than the moonlight hung in the air.

Nine

January 20, 1949. *Snows returned, and winds, over the first half-week, and week, and so on, and so on. Resurgent as great armies of Constantine in their aggression. Nothing less great, or wicked. Temperatures rose and fell, rose and fell, as they do through January, the most wicked weeks of winter in Nebraska. Much of the third week of the New Year of 1949, the temperature remained below zero Fahrenheit, both night and day. On the night of the nineteenth, the mercury dropped to minus twenty-eight,* according to the *Republican.*

Wauneta Sullens had been locked in their house by the snow and ice and her inability to open the front door or one of the windows. She had forgotten not only the dates, but also their meaning.

She could *feel* herself *growing colder.*

* * * * *

"Come home, darling," said the woman in a whisper. "I must be respectable when you get home," she said aloud. Then she giggled and lifted herself, pulling herself up on the last chair at the kitchen table. She had been lying on the floor by the stove on the cushions she had taken from their davenport. The grey cushions bore a Jacquard frieze oak leaf pattern Wauneta had selected in her Sears, Roebuck catalogue in what now seemed an unreal past. They had been settling in, furnishing their first home. She stood and walked to the stove. The young woman washed her face using water she had boiled for drinking.

She took another drink of vodka and turned spritely on her right foot. Drinking had made her enjoy boiling water again. She had grown tired of waiting for water to boil or getting sick, so she had tasted her husband's vodka. She grew to like its taste.

She liked boiling water when she was drinking. She gazed at the roiling water, smiled, and danced slowly as though she was trying to seduce a man or his spirit. She beckoned in the suggestive expressions of her dancing, thrusting her soul upon the evening for the man to see.

The young woman, whose hair had gone gray, heard voices singing *"Deus ex machina,"* and thought the words went pleasantly with the music.

* * * * *

"Who said that?" Wauneta asked loudly. She stopped dancing and stood on the wooden floor of their kitchen.

"Who said that?" she asked again after no one responded.

In the moment it turned into, she had been taken.

Here is where I got lost, she thought, still wondering how she had got by the past few days. Wauneta knew she would endure, but little of what it meant.

Wauneta danced again with the graceful passion of a beautiful woman. She remembered the Lakota dancing at a powwow. She and Robert had driven to the Rosebud reservation across the border into South Dakota. The watched the Indians dance before the firelight in front of their tipis, their village scattered up into the canyon. Wauneta remembered the shadows of Lakota women on the other side of the fire, as though they were dancing with ghosts of ancient gods on the other side of dark hills.

She polished off the vodka the next day.

* * * * *

The winter of 1948–49 is being proclaimed the worst in the history of the western states, wrote the editor of the *Valentine Republican* soberly. *Even old-timers who remembered the blizzard of '88 admitted, after thirteen days of storms, this winter was the worst yet.*

Carrying a wire story, the paper reported, *The 1949 disaster covered a larger area than any other recorded storm, stretching across the country from Canada to Mexico, spanning from the Pacific Ocean to the Missouri River on Nebraska's eastern border. All or part of twelve states suffered from the storms in one way or another. In lower California, which had already suffered a $25 million loss to its $100 million citrus crop, the mercury dropped to 19 degrees.*

Mrs. Carl Wilber received several pictures of the recent California snowstorm from her daughter Mrs. Kenneth Graeff, the local editor recorded. *While the California snowfall was obviously minor compared to what we have experienced, yet it was just as obviously "unusual" for California. Included were pictures of a group of children tobogganing on boards and shovels in a Los Angeles school yard.*

Just as this territory showed signs of returning to normal last weekend, the wind came up again, and all roads were soon blocked once more.

There was light snow Saturday and Sunday and a strong wind which had all roads and the railroad blocked by Saturday afternoon. Winds have blown good-sized rocks onto the snowdrifts.

Snow, stones, wind and drifts! We hope now the weather man has turned his attention elsewhere, and that his fare will be something different for a while, wrote the Crookston correspondent.

Ten

January 27, 1949. The scotch took her longer to drink than the vodka. Wauneta did not like the taste of scotch, and too much would make her sick. She would sit at the wooden table on one of the wooden chairs she had not burned. She sat there, staring at the bottle. The sound of snowmelt dripping through the shingles and boards of the roof, attic, and ceiling had become a drone she no longer noticed. It took her longer to drink scotch. She thought she would never finish the bottle before help arrived or she perished, but help never came, and she survived. The scotch bottles were dry.

Wauneta had been snowed in for nearly a month. She had finished her husband's scotch the previous day, and drank only water from snowmelt. She had boiled water, but it took too long, and she no longer boiled it before drinking.

With methods often resembling ritual, the young woman burned most of the furniture in their living room—everything she could break. She used a kitchen knife to cut upholstery from the frame of the dawn grey davenport with arms of carved mahogany. She burned the wooden frames of the pictures of her family on the walls, and only near the end began removing the glass and burning their photographs. Wauneta burned the oak stand upon which the family Bible rested, leaving the book open on the floor. She changed the chapter every day until she forgot.

* * * * *

Saturday morning it was nice, reported the Republican, *and eight high school boys went south to aid ranchers in clearing the road. At one o'clock, the storm, which had been forecast, hit. The storm forced the boys to give up shoveling. The snow drifted in as fast as they could shovel out.*

With the first prolonged lull in blizzard conditions since the storm first struck this area on the first day of the new year, efforts were being redoubled this week to open the roads or trails to isolated homes in the county where supplies are running low, read the lead under a headline, suggesting a slight fever of urgency. *Many of those homes have been snowbound for almost a month and food and fuel stocks are nearing exhaustion.*

To date, the only means of communication in many cases has been by air. The Valentine Air Service has had two planes in operation continuously, and these were augmented, on Tuesday, by a Prairie Airways plane from Lincoln. Groceries, medicine and fuel oil, in small quantities, are being delivered, but the need now is for heavy fuels in large quantities, which requires that roads be opened.

Under the leadership of County Attorney William B. Quigley, local crews redoubled their efforts to open snow-blocked rural roads.

Eleven

January 30, 1949. Pink light glowed on the snow through the window on the south, but Wauneta did not stand to look at the sunset. The sky in the west resembled a small hurricane, burning in colors from deep blue, nearly black, to illuminated yellow that was nearly white.

From the tabletop on which she was sitting, she could see the pink half-light on the snow outside her window, but it meant little to her.

The great storm clouds in the west cast their menacing pink beauty on the snows, like the first drop of blood in a pool of water. The storm cast clouds as colorful and wonderful as the cascading brilliance of eddies dancing in the springs, radiating light of the summer sun. Wauneta did not remember swimming in the coldness of the springs with her husband in the summer. She did not think of it.

Wauneta Sullens knew nothing of William Quigley's relief efforts. Hope had proved fruitless. Giving up hope put her more at ease, at least for the moment. She had drunk all of her husband's alcohol, and drinking snowmelt no longer bothered her. She could still stand, and sometimes she stood by pulling herself up on the kitchen table. After she had stood, she danced, but usually not very long. She laughed at herself after she danced, because she danced in silly ways that seemed to mean something at the time, but only looked silly as she thought back upon herself and saw herself in her mind, dancing.

Today. *When ghosts ask us to dance, sometimes snows swirl incoherently—congregating with no apparent direction from all corners. Other times, stars stab through night, as though they were lances gleaming in broad daylight. Sometimes, we dance in darkness. We lose ourselves in darkness and do not know we are dancing with ghosts who have asked us to dance. We speak with one another. When we dance in darkness, then, it is most holy. It is as though we are understanding one another, even as we cannot see.*

February 1, 1949. "Break!" said the young woman harshly, yet with only a whisper of breath, into the blackness. "Break!" she repeated several times, sometimes hysterically. She was lying on the floor, unaware that it was the first day of February. She had been trying to break the first leg of their kitchen table for several hours. Somehow she knew the first leg would be most difficult to break.

The fire in the stove was burning low. Embers were glowing and crackling on occasion, but no flames flickered.

Beyond the embers' glow, there was nothing but blackness. Clouds covered the skies. No starlight reached her eyes. Her eyes were blue, but you noticed the red and yellow. Her eyes were red and yellow when she spoke to the table leg, but you could not see the leg of the table. You could see only the glow of the embers in her black pupils, as though she was part of the darkness. She knew someone was watching. She was surrounded by men she had known, and they were watching her, but they would not help. They merely wanted to dance with her.

"Break, you damn thing! Break!" She may have said the word a hundred times to herself, into the blackness.

If she could not break the table leg, the woman knew, she could not put it in the stove. The fire would go out, and she would freeze to death. It would be over.

* * * * *

At last, the woman broke the leg of the kitchen table. She had been using the entire table to stand. Wauneta had burned every other piece of furniture in their house—everything she could break into pieces small enough to shove into the opening of the stove. She had been using the wooden table to stand over the last few days, once she had become too weak to stand on her own. She laboriously lifted herself up onto the tabletop and stood.

Wauneta then threw her arms and neck toward the ceiling and rolled her head on her neck in a slow trance for a few moments, but she suffered acute exhaustion. Her breath nearly gave out. The woman stopped moving and looked at the ceiling before she looked down and threw her weight onto the corner of the table. You heard the breath expelled from the woman. You heard the crack of wood, like a branch snapping in a storm. She had broken off one of the table's legs.

The woman crawled along the floor, dragging the leg of the table. She lifted the wooden leg and put it in the stove. She shoved the leg into the stove as far as it would go. Most of the leg hung from the door of the stove. Embers glowed beneath the wooden leg, as though something had excited them. After the embers had begun to settle again, the woman blew upon the embers, and they glowed more brightly. The young woman blew on the embers, and the embers grew fire, and the flame danced upon the leg of the table. *Salud!* the woman said with a ghost of the gusto of her youth. *Salud.*

Twelve

February 3, 1949. The headline in the *Republican* read, "Army Assumes Gigantic Blizzard Relief Program." *President Truman ordered the Army, Navy and Forest Service to dispatch bulldozers, tractors, Weasels, and other equipment used in Scandinavia during World War II. The army moved into the blizzard disaster area this week with men and equipment to take over the task of opening roads and bringing relief to snowbound families who are suffering for lack of food, fuel and feed for livestock.*

Here in Valentine, they found relief work well underway under the direction of County Attorney William B. Quigley. County Agent R. B. Herrington's aerial reconnaissance indicates all parts of the county appear to have main roads opened, but much hay is covered in all locations. In addition, there seems to be more cases where food and fuel needs are urgent in the west end of the county.

In his weekly report to the district, Senator Hanna wrote, *At 11:30 a.m. January 25, the Governor came before the Legislature, declared an emergency and asked for a half-million dollars for snow removal in about twenty of the worst-affected counties.*

Roads will be opened and emergency needs will be met as rapidly as possible, the local editor concluded. *However, it is asked that no requests be made for emergency help unless an actual emergency, of which there are many, exists.*

We feel quite jubilant. The sun has been shining all day. It isn't blizzarding, although there is one reported to strike this evening, wrote the Kilgore correspondent.

February 9, 1949. Wauneta had been able to stand by pulling herself up on the remains of the cottonwood table in the kitchen. Only one leg now remained with the tabletop. Wauneta could not pull herself up. She could not stand. She could no longer dance.

February 10, 1949. Within a week, *Operation Snowbound,* mentioned by name for the first time in the Valentine newspaper, *was now nearing its mopping-up stage. In less than a week, the United States Army had commenced its work and neared completion. The pride of a nation reminded many of the war we won a few years earlier.*

Engaged in this tremendous operation were 89 pieces of motorized equipment which included 47 bulldozers and also four Weasels now stationed in Valentine, plus trucks and other vehicles. Operating this equipment were 54 army enlisted personnel, 68 civil service personnel, 117 contractors, 12 Navy personnel and 5 Forest Service Employees.

At the latest report, an estimated 2000 miles of roads and trails have been opened in the area, and an average of 250 mile per day in addition were being opened. It was estimated that 150,000 cattle and from 4,000 to 5,000 stacks of hay had been liberated from the drifted snow. In addition, there had been no emergencies reported for several days.

* * * * *

Wauneta lay on the kitchen floor. Her eyes were closed.

* * * * *

Operation Snowbound is doing nicely in the Crookston theatre, said the correspondent there. *Several bulldozers are working to the north and east, and also over in South Dakota in the Lakeview area. To the west, Tom Rasmussen was finally plowed out and he had his pickup to town for the first time Monday. Mrs. Rasmussen reported they were running low on a few items, but with a butchered beef, cream, butter and eggs and a good supply of flour when the storm struck, they fared well.*

The ranchers report that even with a small loss of stock in the area, the weakened condition of the cows will greatly affect the coming calf crop. It probably never will be known just how much the blizzard of '49 will cost the great Sandhills cattle country. The blizzard of 1949 will take its place in history as one of the great storms of the State.

District 37 started school on Tuesday, but the Brownlee school did not open until later, one of the correspondents wrote. *At this time, the oiled roads are open and bulldozers are making roads to individual ranches. Our people took advantage of the first opportunity to secure supplies and food. We are now in comfortable positions,* opined the correspondent from Simeon.

February 11, 1949. *"Operation Snowbound,"* the Wood Lake correspondent heralded on the Friday before publication, *is doing a wonderful job in our community. Most ranchers report that they have been well taken care of and are now able to take care of their stock. They have had an opportunity to replenish their supplies and groceries, fuel and feed. We feel that, in case of another storm, everyone will be better prepared to meet it.*

February 12, 1949. The last time they locked up the young man named Robert Sullens was not the worst.

A number of times, someone had carried Sullens out of the Coachlight and to the county jail for the night, since his wife had been snowed in. Sullens had never had a problem before. He never drank so much that he could not drive the forty-some miles back to his ranch house.

Tonight, it was not that Sullens was too drunk to drive. Nor was Sullens too drunk to walk out of the Coachlight. Those seemed to be the worst nights, the nights he was hardest to reach. He seemed as though he was someplace else those times when they brought him back from the bar.

No, it was more a matter of the deputy tracking down Sullens out in the Sandhills. The young rancher had attempted to walk home a number of times before that hope, too, seemed dashed.

Sheriff Albert Jones was a friend of Sullens. As a friend, he had reached the point where he wanted to let Sullens walk; let him freeze in his own sweat after a day of trudging through the drifts under the sun with no shade.

Let him die. He'll be better off than he is now, the young sheriff thought—words he never uttered. The sheriff did not expect the woman was alive, but he could not explain how smoke still drifted from the stove pipe above the kitchen of the Sullens' ranch house.

Albert Jones knew he could let the man die trying, and he was certain the man would die. The man would be fortunate to die at night, freezing as he slept. It was more likely another storm would strike, as storms had been striking with abandon, after the snow blew in without ceasing the first three days of the year. Another storm would strike, but there would be no flash of lightning, burning life out of the man before he knew it was gone. He would freeze alive.

Sheriff Jones could not let him go, not as an officer of the law. He had stopped chasing down Sullens after the second time he found him, a couple weeks into the storms. Sheriff Jones sent his deputies to stop Sullens. He knew he would be unable to face the man himself. Usually, with the help of a couple ranchers along the route to the Sullens ranch, a deputy would find Robert before he walked too far out of town.

It was the last time Robert Sullens tried to walk home to his wife, stranded there in the middle of the *nether-lands,* as some were calling them. The last time he tried to walk back to his ranch, the county deputy picked him up on a road not far out of town. By then, Sullens had learned the bulldozer would reach Wauneta soon—in a few days—and he did not try to get away from the deputy.

It was the first time he had tried to walk home for a few days. Robert Sullens now walked as though it was what he had done and what he must continue to do, not out of obligation, but from habit. Habit, as we know, lacks passion. Habit does not need passion. It was as though Robert Sullens had calloused himself. He walked.

When the deputy came upon him, Robert Sullens was non-responsive. Walking as though he lacked a mind, the young man was not looking inside, not looking any direction, but ahead.

The deputy came across him on the road and said to the man, "Sullens, I've got to take you back to the jail. Is that okay?"

The young man looked blankly at the deputy. It was not as though he was someplace else; it was as though he had lost all spirit.

Thirteen

February 14, 1949. The headlines and reports jangled in the mind of the young man. He quit listening. He was afraid it would make him crazy. Every person in the county had been rescued, except his wife. By the time the Army bulldozer shoved through the snow on their little road and Robert reached Wauneta, it was Valentine's Day. The metal of his shovel cut into the wood of the door, which was soft with the moisture of melting snow.

February 17, 1949. For the first time since the first edition of 1949, the *Republican's* lead headline had nothing to do with the snowstorm. It read, "Valentine's Day Coronation Highlights Week's Activities."

Friday, Feb. 11, the editor reported, *the mercury launched past 50 for the first time in the new year,* which was no longer new. By Sunday night, the thirteenth, the last night before Robert's shovel dug into the wood of their front door, stars pierced the blackness, and the mercury in the thermometer outside their kitchen window tumbled all the way to nine below, dipping under zero for the final time that winter.

The coronation was declared a success. Eddie Lovejoy, son of Mr. Clyde and Darla Lovejoy of Wood Lake, was crowned King Badger, and Abigail Abbott, daughter of Dr. William and Cecilia Abbott of Brownlee, was crowned his Queen.

Below the fold on the front page, the headline announced, "Army Completes Road Breaking." *The army reached the end of its task in this area early this week, and demobilization began at Midnight on Monday,* after the last crew brought in Wauneta Sullens.

Although not all the roads in the county had been opened, the task had been advanced to the point where most farmers and ranchers can now carry on without undue hardship.

Practically all residents of the county are now able to get out for supplies.

Fourteen

February 14, 1949. The young man held his wife. He was sitting on the floor of their kitchen, holding her beside the remains of the table he had made from the old cottonwood. If he eased his grasp for an instant, the woman would tug at him with her hands and whimper.

"Wauneta, I have to carry you to the snowplow," the young man said.

* * * * *

"I have to let go so I can stand up," he said slowly when she did not say anything.

She looked up at his eyes.

"I have to stand and carry you to the snowplow," the young man said again slowly, and loudly, like he wanted her to understand him in a language she did not know.

She released her clutch.

"Will you help me lift her?" the young man asked the snowplow driver.

"I will," the man said. "I'm sorry, Mr. Sullens."

"Thank you," the young rancher said. "Please help me lift her."

February 17, 1949. *Operation Snowbound was brought to a close in this area Monday at midnight. This was a wonderful service made possible by the U.S. Army Engineers. Without a doubt, it kept stock losses down much lower than otherwise could have been expected. Much needed feed was made accessible only by powerful bulldozers. Many miles of roads also were opened by the same means. The ranchers who were helped by one or more of the fleet of bulldozers say, "Hats off" to the United States Army Engineers,* wrote the Crookston correspondent, her last account of the storm.

It was nice to see a few bare spots of the good earth for a change. Hope we've had our quota of snow from this winter.

February 14, 1949. The bulldozer carried Wauneta and her husband down the path the men had cleared on the seven miles of trail road to the highway. The narrow road looked like a fingernail scraped into the surface of grandmother's ice cream, fresh from the hand churn, if you were hovering where vultures were circling. The bulldozer crawled along the path in the snow, through the remains of the institution of nature that had reigned for six weeks.

Only the driver looked out at the road. The young woman would not open her eyes.

Today. The rest of what happened to Wauneta and Robert Sullens is a tale of tragedy that I tried to spare you. Wauneta was institutionalized at her own request before winter began that year, near the end of 1949. She was put away in a sanatorium.

Wauneta Sullens lived the remainder of her life behind the walls, windows, and bars of the Rosebud Sanatorium in Rapid City, South Dakota. She lived there along with a few other white women like her—women suffering from different mental illnesses—and many men, women, and children dying of tuberculosis.

Yesterday. *These years were the worst in its history,* or so say our historians. The stately red brick building, constructed proudly on a hilltop, began as a boarding school for brainwashing indigenous children in 1898. *Sioux. Shoshone. Flathead. Crow. Cheyenne. Arapaho.* American! American! The native children shall be American!

Before the *worst years in its history,* children were dragged kicking and screaming in Lakota's several dialects—and other native languages—into the government's stately brick building to be indoctrinated in the *white man's way of life.* Abuse, neglect, and death were more prominent than the spirits of their fathers—spirits the children were forced to repent of. Repent! Repent! Repent of your language, or we will cut out your tongue.

* * * * *

These years were the worst in its history, worse than the years of brainwashing the children. These were the years of performing experiments on the children we had brainwashed and who had contracted tuberculosis in our schools.

* * * * *

> *Experimental procedures were tested on the tuberculosis patients. The disease spread like wildfire with no cure in sight. Although sanitariums were considered to be the most advanced treatment centers for TB patients, the treatments were brutal and grisly at best.*
>
> *All the doctors could do was try experimental surgeries. Many patients went insane or committed suicide. In all, death was prominent. The patients were rarely outside, and many were simply left in rocking chairs.*

* * * * *

We know little of Wauneta Sullens, other than the pieces we see in her records from the sanatorium. The medical records of Wauneta Sullens bear little scrutable witness to the words in her mind.

December 31, 1950. Robert sat down alone at the table he had made from the fallen cottonwood tree in the yard—the same old cottonwood he used to make the first table. He had to make three new legs for it. On the table was a small bucket of ice that he had pulled from the edges of the horse tank outside the barn and a tumbler into which he had thrown a few chunks. From a bottle of cheap scotch, he poured himself a drink. He had bought the bottle from a store he had begun frequenting only recently. On his way out, Robert was saying something to the proprietor and, not watching where he was going, and he tripped over the leg of a Native American who had passed out by the doorway. Robert Sullens looked and saw it was a good friend from high school.

Fifteen

July 14, 1986. Old Robert Sullens finally had no choice but to stop. His new young neighbor was parked nearly in the middle of the trail road that connected their ranches. The man was standing outside the door of his truck. The old man had no choice but to say hello to the young man who had moved in at the next ranch over. He had come there with his wife about a year before.

Robert Sullens, who had lived like a recluse for nearly forty years, did not know the couple had a newborn. They had passed each other on the road a few times a month, but Mr. Sullens had never stopped to talk. It was not his habit. The young man had stopped a couple times before, but the old man just drove by slowly, courteously. He did not look the young man in the eyes.

Finally, the old rancher had no choice but to stop. The young neighbor had parked his truck in the middle of the road.

Robert Sullens's white hair was neatly cut and pressed by sweat and the base of the crown of the cowboy hat he had removed from his head. His hat was on the bench seat of his old Chevy, on the seat next to him.

They young man introduced himself, and Robert Sullens did the same. The young man surprised Mr. Sullens by asking him about 1948 at some point in their conversation. The two talked for a spell.

"What'd you say your name was?" the old man asked after a point.

"Call me Masick," the young man said. The old man's eyes were charcoal gray, almost smoky.

"Masick?" repeated the old man with a face wrinkled and reddened by years on the range, squinting at the young man slightly cockeyed. "That your first name, or your last?"

"First name, sir," the young man said to him with a thick Southern accent. "Masick Jammers."

An early reviewer asked me to write a short story about my novel Tumbleweed Lexicon. *The following essay is what became of that suggestion. I provide all of Juanita Sullens's actual history, at least from the records I have been able to discover. In the essay, I also explain why I wrote* Snowbound. *I did not set out intending to include Crazy Horse in the essay. The mind is a puzzling device.*

JUANITA SULLENS: AN ESSAY ON THE ART OF CHANGING FACES

When I was a boy, my mother told me the story of Juanita Sullens. It is a story worthy of being told. I finally got around to writing a novel that emanates hazily from that story. After my father died ten years ago, I wrote a novel based loosely on Father's grim last months. It was the first novel I wrote. I wrote the story of my father for myself. I wrote a story about Wauneta Sullens for my mother. I gave little thought to why I spelled the woman's name as *Wauneta*. It is, in fact, Juanita Sullens. I don't know where the misspelling came from. For many years, I thought it might perhaps be the town of Wauneta that got me spelling it that way. Southeast of where I grew up is a town in Chase County called Wauneta. My parents took my sister and me to a farm down the Frenchman Valley from Wauneta to acquire a couple of puppies when I was about ten. As far as the farmer who bred them could figure, they were part Border Collie and part coyote. I always liked the name of the town. It was pretty in a sad kind of way and seemed to go with the woman I always imagined: Wauneta Sullens. It was only recently that I learned from where else the misspelling might have come.

What I want to tell you now is what, in fact, happened to Juanita Sullens, according to everything in reported history. Juanita Sullens was born and died and had been married to someone. She was not married to *Robert Sullens*, as I call him in my novel. She was married to Mike. There is no further recorded history of the woman, with one exception.

Single Source

I do not pretend to be a historian. I lack the patience for details demanded by science. All I will report I learned from my mother Beverly Pollock. Mother's maiden name was Buck. She had known the woman, Mrs. Sullens. I searched, with help from a librarian friend, and found the little you already know: Juanita Sullens was born, she was married, and she died. From my mother I learned more.

Juanita Sullens was snowed in alone in her ranch house during the Great Blizzard of 1949. According to my mother, Mrs. Sullens and her husband ranched and lived near the heart of Cherry County, many miles from Valentine. Juanita's husband was in Valentine getting groceries and supplies or something from somewhere we must suppose from all known accounts. He was away from home when the snow struck.

[Stop. Please pull up a map of the Sandhills. A satellite view is best. See the hills, rippling like an ocean floor. Those are the Sandhills: vast, hardly populated. Find the town of Valentine and drag your finger down south, halfway through the county. That's where Juanita was. The nearest neighbors were not a mile away, which might shock some of my city readers. They were not two miles away. The nearest occupied ranch house was several miles away.]

In the past twenty-some years, I have traveled to Cherry County three or four times a year for fishing, hiking, writing, and putting on a marathon that attracts runners from all over the country to Nebraska. In recent years, after coming upon the idea of writing a story set in the Sandhills during the Great Blizzard, I have sat at bars and kitchen tables, taking oral histories from some of the old ranchers about the storm. Some remember details vividly—names, sounds, wonders—but none recall Juanita Sullens. My mother is the only person I have found who remembers the story. It has remained constant. When Mother told me the story the first time, it left an impression. I remember being haunted by the story of Juanita Sullens that my mother told me when I was very young. I was probably too young to have heard such a story. It was too scary for me. It frightened me. I was old enough, clearly, to have fathomed the story, or it would not have struck me, but I do not remember how old I was. Nor does my mother.

My mother told me that Mr. Sullens was away getting groceries or supplies or something. She thought he had probably driven to Valentine. At a minimum, we must presume that Mr. Sullens got to Valentine eventually. Mr. Sullens was a long way from home—two dozen miles from Juanita—when the snowstorm hit the Nebraska Sandhills with its evil and unexpectedly brutal punch. It was the beginning of the new year.

I assume Mr. Sullens was racing the storm to town to get groceries and supplies before the storm hit. A blizzard hit the Sandhills back in November, and the Sullens were snowbound for a week. I imagine Mr. Sullens remembering November and racing for town, frustrated and fighting.

I learned in my first few years of railroad litigation, when I was a young lawyer, that you don't race trains. The storm was much larger than a train.

Snowbound

If you have not read a little about the Great Blizzard of 1949, I recommend the book by Roy Alleman, an excellent documentary produced by Wyoming PBS, or the sobering historical reporting the *Omaha World-Herald* responsibly publishes regularly. All offer accurate and detailed historical accounts.

The most colorful historical accounts come from local correspondents who reported into the *Valentine Republican.* The correspondents, most unidentified other than by the village for which they reported, provide true color, hinting at the rawest emotional responses to the devastation, but all of the local correspondents couch their commentary in a tone gravitating toward hope. They performed their duty with discipline and honesty. We must inspire ourselves with hope if we are to overcome what we face. That remains true.

The stories we read speak of restoration and recovery—of clawing back. Alleman alone is honestly gruesome in his description, and then only sparingly. He, too, was disciplined, though much less orthodox. Alleman's account of the storm was grand in painting the vastness, the breadth of the storm, and its beginning and ending. With finer strokes, he paints the horrible echoing in between.

The Great Blizzard of 1949 was of epic proportions. I use *epic* in the true sense of the word, the sense that Alleman so correctly painted, not the trite and hackneyed manner in which the word is idiomatically used these days. The storm did more than strike, it lingered. It was.

Indeed, periodically, we must be reminded not only of nature's majesty, but also her cruelly grinding might. The reminders warn us, but nothing reminds us of the cruel might of nature more than death, devastation, and suffering.

The past will never shield us from the present. We face our own battles. I think of the 2019 winter floods that dragged ice and sand across cornfields, swept away bridges and dams that were in disrepair, and drowned calves as they fell from their mothers in the east and froze them in the west. Today's stories will be sung someday. Today they are being reported with accuracy and good color. There is a reason we should be thankful for modern technology. The victims of the floods of 2019 tell the stories themselves, and the local newspaper coverage is good.

For that we should be thankful. For the words of the local correspondents during the time of the Great Blizzard of 1949, we must be thankful, and there is no disputing the value of the work of Mr. Alleman, and the historical accounts I have mentioned from reputable sources.

Today, though, we should be glad we see the grimmer pictures. I will not describe the pictures here more than I have already. You can read the news accounts and personal postings of the cyclonic storms of 2019. Much like those, the 1949 blizzards hit repeatedly, in rhythms, with nearly mythological ferocity.

The snows of 1949 socked in twelve states and spoiled fruit crops in California. Children in Los Angeles tobogganed on shovels and boards. The storms did not relent for nearly a month. Winter's rhythms brought more winds and snows, drifting over roads within hours after men had cleared them.

Hay was dropped to cattle by airplane during the blizzards of 1949 just as it was during the 2019 winter floods. Food was dropped to ranch houses. Railroad tracks were cleared by the heroic efforts of local men and boys with nothing else to do. I have heard the account of one of the boys myself. He was fourteen when he helped dig out a locomotive near Merriman. Yet many ranchers remained stranded. Livestock continued to perish in the grimmest of ways. Life seemed to be ending.

Critique

I was surprised at first that the *Valentine Republican* editor provided the color from California—the children tobogganing. The news item appeared early during the storm, when it was at the peak of its gruesome devastation—the sudden volume of snow, the cold, and the winds hammering and hammering and hammering (like a longed-for Oxford comma). It was a light-hearted wire clip—a clumsy distraction. The editor left us no feel for the local weight of the storm.

I have little regard for the editor of the *Valentine Republican.* It was as though he did not comprehend the monster that had swallowed the Sandhills, or even take it seriously. He certainly did little to tell its story. I hope I do not offend the honor of my father, who with my mother published and edited the bi-weekly *Keith County News,* or my grandfather, who also was an editor and publisher, or my friends who are editors and publishers today, including the editor and publisher of the journal to which I am submitting this essay for favorable consideration. You tell us stories, all of those I have named or otherwise identified. The stories written by the editor of the *Valentine Republican* did nothing but report the facts, and reported little but the very general facts surrounding the storm—roads closed and dances cancelled, and children sledding in southern California.

Journalists must tell us stories.

What was happening to Juanita Sullens? What was going on?

United States Army

Nebraska was losing its struggle against the storm of 1949. Things were going very badly. It was nearing the end of January, and many ranchers remained snowbound and were running short on food and fuel. Their businesses were failing. Cattle were beginning to perish in larger numbers. Before long, calving would begin in earnest. The situation was not critical yet, but it was getting close.

Nebraska Governor Val Peterson, whose grandson currently serves as state Attorney General, prevailed upon President Harry S. Truman to send in the United States Army with equipment engineered for fighting in Scandinavia during World War II. On January 24, 1949, President Truman commenced *Operation Snowbound*.

Juanita Sullens remained stranded for more than three weeks.

I am not certain Mr. Sullens would agree with what I said earlier about racing the train. Being hit by a locomotive would have put an end to it for him.

The Buck Family

By some accounts, my mother's father, Glenn Buck, was a short-tempered and feisty cuss. Reportedly, Grandpa was not shy about throwing a verbal or political punch. That will not surprise my friends. Most people who spoke to me about Grandpa liked him, but not all. Few now living remember him. Grandpa probably had reason to be a little cockier than I can afford to be. Grandpa Buck acquired a ranch in the Sandhills from his predecessor as editor-publisher of the *Nebraska Farmer,* Governor Samuel McKelvie. What matters now, though, is that Grandpa raised Hereford cattle on the ranch next to Mike and Juanita Sullens.

Mother told me the story of Juanita Sullens when I was a boy. It was a memory from her own girlhood. Weather has been a fascination of my mother's for as long as I can remember. She and my father published the *Keith County News,* and we lived above a siltstone beach on the south side of Lake McConaughy, a reservoir on the North Platte River in western Nebraska, near the corner of the Panhandle. On a daily basis, Mother has recorded weather and conditions of the lake, including when the ice covered the lake and finally melted every year. Mother did not like when the lake was idle. She once said idleness was bad for the mind.

Mother grew up in Lincoln. Grandpa Buck took the family to spend summers and holidays on his ranch in Cherry County. He told my mother and her sister and brother how to raise cattle and care for them and love the Sandhills. He taught them all the things good ranchers teach their children. Grandpa even taught mother the Latin names of the grasses.

Convergence

I know the grasses only by their common names, like blue grama and side-oats grama. I remember blue grama because it reminds me of a toothbrush, and I remember side-oats grama because it looks like a Sioux war spear. When I was a boy, I knew it only that way—*war spear*—but I recognized the grass. I would lie in the grasses south of Lake McConaughy, where I grew up, and look at the birds flying wildly in the windy blue sky, and I felt the grasses brush against me. I pretended I was Crazy Horse. I pretended I was the great Sioux shaman.

Crazy Horse

Crazy Horse, if you will pardon the diversion, had his vision in the Nebraska Sandhills. His vision became his name. The boy in his visions saw his life laid out in front of him, and he walked that path, and we wonder why his fate was strangely similar to his vision. He saw something coming that we cannot see. Crazy Horse had higher powers. Those powers led him to be a great shaman warrior. Based on the evidence before me, that is what I believe. I believe in the shaman of many religions, although I do not profess to follow all religions. I think it would be impossible, frankly, but I am not here to talk religion—or politics, which is my day job.

Crazy Horse was a young teenager when he was camping with his Brulé relatives along the Blue Water Creek, about thirty minutes up the North Platte River from where I was lying in the grama grasses. I did not know all the stories yet, but was imagining my own. Thirty minutes and more than 120 years separated us. I was Crazy Horse, thirteen, lying in the grasses blowing against my pale, freckled cheeks, imagining I was an Oglala. The town where I went to high school was named for that tribe, in its honor.

Crazy Horse was a boy—twelve or thirteen—camped with his uncle's tribe, the Brulé Sioux, along the Blue Water, a tributary flowing south into the North Platte. At the time, the boy had experienced his vision, but had not yet been given the name by which we know him. He was called Curly, for his wavy and light-colored hair. Curly and some friends—perhaps cousins—rode their ponies upstream to the headwaters of the Blue Water. If you have not been to the headwaters of the Blue Water and you are within driving distance, then shame on you, if I may use the phrase my Grandma Buck would have used.

Grandma Buck, *lingering on in her pale blue eyes,* I believe, fancied herself as Japanese. In portraits, Grandma appeared in Japanese attire. In one set of photographs, she was holding an Oriental fan. She had two photographs with the fan. In one, the fan was closed compactly. It looked more like a pencil or a comb than a fan. In the next, the fan was opened. I always thought of butterflies when I looked at that picture.

Don't get me wrong. I have great fondness for my grandmother. I knew her only after a stroke had twisted her body, slurred her speech, and made living difficult. She was determined to be beautiful, and she was. She has mannerisms and common twists of language I have spun through my novel. In the novel, for example, Wauneta Sullens is blonde, but believes she has dark hair, even before the snowstorm hit.

The mind is a puzzling device. *Down for you is up.*

Crescent Lake

Which brings me back to Crazy Horse, or Curly. He and his friends, all young teenagers, were hunting near the headwaters of the Blue Water, probably for waterfowl. If you have not been to the headwaters of Blue

Water Creek, you have not been to the Crescent Lake National Wildlife Reserve, which protects a wonder of nature. The lake is another large puddle of the Ogallala Aquifer, but one with an unusually large and diverse population of wildlife. Ancient winds formed sand dams across the Blue Water, creating a large, sustainable confluence between ground and surface water. Everything about this place is fascinating; I've found an arrowhead in a blowout near the modern banks of the lake and seen trumpeter swans and other birds of the refuge.

Under a broad blue sky last autumn, when wild sunflowers were in full golden bloom, I drove a longtime friend through the Crescent Lake Reserve on our way to a funeral in Oshkosh. We had been fishing on a river in the Sandhills. My friend is an avid outdoorsman. He remarked, as we were driving through the vast, isolated preserve, that he had seen more species of waterfowl in thirty minutes than he had seen in his fifty years.

I told my friend the story of Crazy Horse and the Blue Water, after we were downstream from the reserve, on our way to the funeral of a local banker, who was as fine a man as western Nebraska has raised. His name is Bill Olson, and he took my father and me goose hunting every Thanksgiving morning for many years during my childhood and early adult years. Bill's nephew took me bird hunting near Lake Crescent when we were young.

When Curly was a young teenager, he was riding back with his friends from the lakes and reedy wetlands—what is now protected in the reserve. The boys' hunt was, in all likelihood, bountiful. Curly and the other young Lakota were probably celebrating their skills and their bounty on a warm autumn afternoon trot the twenty-seven-or-so miles back to camp. The broad sky stretched in all directions, but the southeast, back toward camp, was blue and clear.

The sky to the southeast was hazy. As they rode on, the Indian boys saw that the haze emanated from a few plumes of smoke. As they rode further into the hills, they saw the plumes of smoke came from their camp. The other boys rode west to another camp, away from the fires at their own camp. Curly rode alone to the Blue Water.

The boy walked his pony into the cool darkness of the valley, smoke clinging to the thick river valley air. The boy came upon the burning remains of the camp. Tipis, weapons, dolls, and other belongings had been pushed into piles and were smoldering. Crazy Horse walked through the camp and looked at the bodies. He came upon the living and the dead. He saw an old woman—a Cheyenne—with her intestines hanging out. She was still alive. He saw more than one girl with her pubis scalped.

It is less painful to forget the past, but we must be reminded.

Christmas at the Ranch

The Buck family spent the holidays at their ranch house in the Sandhills during the winter of 1948–49. Mother and her brother celebrated Christmas and rang in the new year with Grandma and Grandpa in their ranch house in the Sandhills.

Grandpa caught wind that a storm was brewing. Home, work, and school were in Lincoln. He told my mother and uncle about a blizzard that hit the Sandhills in November. Their neighbors, the Sullens, had been snowed in at their ranch for almost a week. Grandpa gave instructions, and the children helped prepare for their rapid departure. Mother remembers pouring kerosene in the toilets so the water would not freeze.

With their chores complete, Grandpa loaded up the family, and they drove from the ranch, heading out on the long sand trail road leading to Highway 20. The family sped back to Lincoln. My mother remembers watching the storm clouds coming behind them. She and her brother watched out the rear window of Grandpa's Thunderbird. Mom was twelve at the time.

The storm descended ruthlessly on the Sandhills.

Juanita Sullens

Juanita Sullens was stranded on the second day of 1949. Storms continued slamming the Sandhills, relentless in their fury. The US Army was sent in. Near the time *Operation Snowbound* was winding down—the last of the roads cleared—Mr. Sullens finally reached Juanita. It was the middle of February. (We must imagine, as my novel imagines, what it was like.) She had been stranded alone since the beginning of the year. Juanita Sullens was alive, but she had lost her mind.

According to my mother, Juanita was eventually committed to a sanatorium in South Dakota. She never returned. Mother does not know how long Juanita lived in the sanatorium. Grandpa had kept in touch with Mr. Sullens for some time after the storm, but eventually lost track of him.

Blue Water

Learning of Crazy Horse and the Battle of Bluewater from the likes of Mari Sandoz, R. Eli Paul, Paul N. Beck, Dennis Shimmin, and my own newspaper-publisher father helped me imagine the mind of Wauneta Sullens. Hearing their words helped me fill in the parts of the story my mother could not remember—the parts, in almost all probability, that no one knew or recorded. Their words and others somehow helped me write the fictional account of a different story.

Long before I had read anything about the Indian wars—I was a young boy—my father took me to the battle site. Dennis Shimmin was the local game and parks superintendent at Ash Hollow State Historical Park, where General William Harney and his troops camped the night before the battle. Mr. Shimmin guided us over private land to the site of the battle.

Mr. Shimmin and my father told me about the battle, how the infantry marched up the canyon, and the cavalry flanked the east side of the valley, behind the hills, beyond the Indian scouts, out of sight. Other than the sound of the horses' hooves plunging through the grasses and soft sand, the cavalry rode silently. Mr. Shimmin and Dad told me of the parley, of the battle, of soldiers firing at Indians huddled under ledges of sandstone.

We had such a ledge within ten yards of my bedroom window. The Indian women and their babies trembled under the outcropping as coward soldiers hung their pistols down and fired blindly. I was afraid to go under the sandstone ledge near my house. I had always been afraid of the rattlesnakes. The Indians knew where rattlesnakes lived. My young mind went places that disturbed me.

Neither Mr. Shimmin nor my father told me what the soldiers did to the people they had killed. I read about that later. Still, it is all one story, and I would not know it as I do without learning all the stories myself. Others have told me their understandings of the battle and its various elements. I am grateful to all of them. I will tell you briefly about the battle.

With a reputation for being "prolific in the use of profanity," General Harney parleyed under a cottonwood with the village leader, Little Thunder, but the palaver was nothing more than a feint. The general was buying time for his cavalry. He could not know their whereabouts precisely. That, and surely Harney did not want the Indians to think he was in a hurry or to suspect he planned to attack.

The general wanted the Indians to be surprised by his attack, but the scarcity of trees along the small creek made it impossible not to be seen marching up the valley.

The false parley was at last abandoned. Little Thunder and a few other Brulé men began to walk back toward their tribe.

Rewind: The Mormon Cow Incident

The substance of the false parley was itself largely manufactured. It is a long, tangled story. I will spare you but a few details.

A little more than a year before, a cow from a Mormon wagon train wandered into a Brulé Sioux camp on the North Platte River, far upstream from the Blue Water, into what is now Wyoming. A Miniconjou Sioux man, visiting the kindred Brulé, killed the cow, and (historians surmise) the Indians ate it.

The cow's owner reported the incident to an officer of US Army at Fort Laramie, not far up the river. The same day, the Brulé chief, Conquering Bear, reported the incident to the same officer at the Fort. Conquering Bear offered to pay for the cow, but the officer insisted that the Indian who had killed the cow must be turned over for proper disciplinary proceedings. Conquering Bear walked away.

Clumsily leading another ill-fated parley was Lieutenant Grattan, a greenhorn. John Lawrence Grattan, a brevet second lieutenant fresh out of the middle of the class at West Point, was dispatched from the Fort to the camp of Brulé led by Conquering Bear. Lieutenant Grattan's sole charge was to return with the suspected cow killer.

Grattan arrived, set up a cannon or two, summoned the Indian leaders to parley, and demanded that Conquering Bear turn over the killer of the Mormon cow. Conquering Bear told Grattan (with an honesty we should emulate) that the killer was visiting from a different tribe, and the chief had no jurisdiction to force the man to do anything. Grattan persisted with his demand. Conquering Bear told the young officer he could go find the suspect in the camp himself, and then Conquering Bear walked away.

The first and only shot from the cannon mortally wounded Conquering Bear. The soldiers did not have time to reload before all men and boys of the Brulé village, and many of the women, had run to the cannons. (It pains me to admit that I always find that part funny, perhaps in a Freudian way.) Grattan had positioned his cannons too close to the camp. He and his small force of soldiers were summarily massacred.

According to Sandoz, Curly was in Conquering Bear's camp when the chief was hit by the cannon fire. The camp was moved east and south, along the North Platte River and down into Nebraska. Curly, not yet a teenage boy, was in Conquering Bear's tent and watched him dying. After seeing the old man's yellow face and hollow, far-away eyes, Curly left the camp on his pony. He was alone for several days in the Nebraska Sandhills and did not eat or drink. It was then that the boy had his vision.

A Recipe and Ghosts

Months later, when General Harney visited the Brulé camp and feigned parley with Little Thunder, the general purported to be seeking those responsible for the Grattan massacre after the Mormon cow incident. The General demanded that Little Thunder turn over the men.

Immediately on the bootheels of his false parley, Harney led a massacre of his own, killing eighty-six and taking the remaining seventy hostage. General Harney's troops marched the Sioux, mostly women and children, back to their camp in Ash Hollow. Behind him, in the valley of the Blue Water, Harney left the dead and the scalped, half of them women and children, as well as a few living to die.

A boy named Curly found them.

* * * * *

The story of Juanita Sullens has haunted me since I was a boy. I wondered what became of Juanita, and of Mr. Sullens. Besides my mother, no one else I have encountered remembers the story, or even the name. I found little in the newspapers or libraries. My friend at the library helped me find Juanita Sullens's grave.

My mother has long loved cooking. She remains an excellent chef, one of the finest and most creative I know. Mom has an extensive collection of old recipes. Included in her collection is the only written record I have discovered that tells a story about Juanita Sullens. The record is a recipe of Mrs. Sullens herself.

At the top of the recipe card, in my mother's handwriting, are the words "BEST Oatmeal Cookies." At the bottom of the card, my mother wrote in her precise cursive, "Wauneta Sullens—ranch wife."

JANUS: TALES OF ANTS AND SNAKES AND GROWING UP IN RURAL KEITH COUNTY

How wrong I was. Two-headed monster of my imagination. Sun, burning like the eye of a buffalo.

Walking up from the lake near our house on the south edge of the Sandhills, I came upon two garter snakes, fighting with their necks tangled. Everything about them was mad: two mad, black flicking tongues and jaws so wide I thought they would flap backwards. Their arched fangs startled me. I was not watching a scrimmage on the grounds outside school; it was a death match.

It seemed as though the snakes were two brothers fighting. Their colorful stripes looked identical, and their heads were the same shape and size. I stopped and watched the two snakes fighting for a while.

What I had been doing, I don't remember. It was hot—summer. School was out. I would be in eighth grade. The junior high was in town. Still riding with Dad every morning to school.

In summer, sometimes Dad drove me to the golf course, where I would walk and play until he was done working at the newspaper. A couple times, I played fifty-four holes in a day. Those were the days when I was not skipping stones on Lake McConaughy, catching crawdads or fish, or burning red ants with a magnifying glass.

Following one ant-burning ritual, I was walking up the steps of our house. A hostile ant had stowed away in my under pants and clenched my testicles in its poisoned jaws.

I ran up the remaining stairs and into my parents' bedroom. It was mid-afternoon, so no one would be there. I yanked off my shorts and white briefs and did to myself what you do to yourself when an ant is biting you. I was swatting and swatting at it as hard as I dared until it finally released. I looked up and saw my mother looking at me and holding a basket of laundry.

* * * * *

I spent much time hiking around the cliffs at the lake when I was a boy. I was not frightened of snakes until I was older.

Even now, when I return home, where I qualify for the senior discount at the golf course, I remain frightened of snakes. When I hike in the canyons of western Nebraska, I think of snakes. Yet I no longer want to run from them, like I did for a time.

I remain scared of snakes. I will not hold one, not even a garter snake. In the real world, I am not fearful. I don't spend my time worrying about snakes any more than I worry about mountain lions. I am careful where I step and put my hands, but I don't worry much about where I walk or hike. I will not let a snake limit my adventures. I have to go somehow. There is no good way to go. You have to face it.

When I was a young boy, I did not care about snakes. I roamed with abandon. I don't remember thinking about where snakes might lurk, not until fifth grade. Before that, I would hike and climb the siltstone cliffs along Lake McConaughy. Rattlers find homes under shelves on the cliffs. I did not think about snakes, and I didn't watch for snakes, and I did not care.

Janus and I were the only fifth graders. We were wandering around the grade school grounds looking for branches for a science project. There was one elm tree on the quarter section of school land, and it was on the other side of the school. I don't recall whether idle minds or some fancy led us the long way around the one-room schoolhouse toward the tree in search of small branches.

I spotted a stick and reached to retrieve it. I never remembered what else I was doing. Chattering with Janus about something, perhaps. We were good friends. She proved me wrong when I argued like a boy who can't be wrong about anything, including which edge of the knife was sharp. I drew the blade across the pale, thin skin of my palm until blood drew its own line.

Janus, the girl whose name I sang to myself when I wandered through the canyons at the lake. This was back in the days before you wondered much about love or anything except looking for whatever you were looking for and finding pleasure you did not understand in words and snail fossils.

Whatever we were chattering about blended with sunshine, breezes from directions of which, like grammar, we cared little, and the rest of the ground around the branch when it, at last, came into focus. Before me, coiled, the largest rattlesnake I had seen showed its angry fangs and flicked its mad black tongue. It flicked its tongue at me.

My face was within a foot of the rattler. I had surprised it. The snake had no time to rattle its warning.

I do not know if snakes are angry when they fight other snakes or attack men, but they look angry. Knowing Janus Wi Buffalo was standing behind me, I leapt over the snake without thinking, shouted something to Janus, and ran around the school to meet her on the front steps.

Our teacher called Gib Jasnoch, the farmer whose daughter, Melinda, wrote to me what I thought was my first love letter. I called her to discuss it after finding the note folded in one of my books. She told me she had written it for a class. The Jasnochs' house was across the gravel road, a quarter mile exactly to the east. They were the closest house to the school by a few miles.

Mr. Jasnoch ambled into the schoolhouse, grinning. He held a spade in his hand. Mr. Jasnoch asked me where the snake was. I took him outside to show him. He did not find the snake, but he told me I did a good job.

I do not know whether the rattler struck at me or ever died. I did not think much about it until I came upon the two garter snakes fighting when I was in junior high. At last, the two snakes had begun to bore me. They were not going to kill each other. I poked at them with a stick. I saw it was not two snakes, but one snake with two long necks and heads.

* * * * *

I remain frightened of snakes, but not like I was after seeing the twins playing and for many years after. I remain aware that I will not live forever. I don't know if that is why I no longer want to kill snakes when I see them.

WIDOWER: A POEM ABOUT GOOSE HUNTING IN GARDEN COUNTY

The measure of a man
Can be seen in how he sees God's land,
All its creatures
And the metaphors he finds.

The walk to the goose pit always wakes the hunter:
The cold, an unseen chorus of ganders and hens,
The blended smell of native grasses on wet valley air,
A coyote scampering to distant hazy hills,
The sun over the far end of a fencerow,
Glowing, wicking red up a cumulus wall,
Soon to eclipse, soon to make easier
The sighting of birds to the east.

I grab a whiskbroom from our pit
And dust the river's breath
Frozen on the decoys.
The widower lights his stove
And unloads the eggs and bacon,
Coffee and bread we packed in.
Doc has cooked for four kids,
And I trust him with a skillet.

The aroma of our breakfast rises, and
It's almost as though it stirs the geese on the refuge,
Their chorus sharpening to a chaotic pitch.
I watch the way of the refrain and soon see rise

A little flock, ten or fifteen small birds,
Flighty and unnerved.
A dozen or so up in front, to the north.
No sooner have I spoken than they turn upriver.
They're heading west.

You never hope for a bird to fall too early in the morning.
There is breakfast, there is the wonder of the morning:
An eagle rousing uneasy waterfowl,
The first eastbound coal train,
The stillness,
Your breath on the tailwind of an eastern storm,
Draining the first cup of coffee,
Hoping flocks stay settled for the moment
As the stream steams. We make
the same exchanges every hunt: the weather,
Which brings all men together—
A simple subject, but perhaps the only one
We so fully share—our families, our jobs,
The election just past, the bowl game to come,
The economy, disharmony in foreign lands,
Past hunts: when the birds flew,
How we braved the finger-numbing cold,
Birds we took home, birds that got away,
As if
They were ours.

There's two in the east, four-o'clock,
The eye doc breaks in.
I see them.
We roll close the hay-covered lid of the pit
And watch through small cracks.
We call, and the morning beyond fades
Into our minds. Whispering, tracking
The course of our two prey,
Their guttural honking voices passed
Winter upon winter.

The Canadas circle lazily behind us,
Then set their wings. The morning
Disappears in our racing hearts.
The calling ends, and we crane
Our necks, slowly, clumsily as
The pair circles west and north
With heads turned, long straight necks,
Beaks pointed toward our decoys, ever
Losing altitude. Gander and hen
So close you hear the rush of air
On their wings and chests, see
The white saddles under their chins
And gleams of the full sky's light
In their eyes. You marvel at the beauty.
Turning back west sharply, they break
Their winds and drop their black webfeet
For the final flapping descent.

Take 'em,
Doc shouts in a whisper.
I throw open the lid, and
Two blasts blast back to back.
One bird falls.
Doc lowers his gun. I take
One more parting shot
At the bird that got away.
Nice shot, Doc. Let me get your bird.

Wait.

I follow Doc's gaze to the east
And see the new single flying rapidly away,
Before turning back to begin
Nearly the same circle he had begun with his mate.
We duck low but do not close the pit.
For a moment morning returns.
Setting down his shotgun,
Doc watches the single and beyond.

They mate for life,
He says. I listen.
Sometimes they fly on
For years alone.
Sometimes they come right back
Like this one,
But they mate for life.

On May 9, 2019, our daughter Katie performed with other fine arts students on the stage in the Milford High School Auditorium. Of course, Katie sang beautifully and the whole performance was excellent, but a Japanese exchange student stole the show without realizing it. I got home that night and couldn't help but write about the experience. I sent a copy to the local weekly, The Milford Times, *telling them if they had any space to fill, they were welcome to use it. The editor published it with a wonderful spread of photographs.*

MHS FINE ARTS PUTS ON REMARKABLE SEASON FINALE: THE STORY OF HANANO IWATSUKI

The Milford High School Fine Arts Department performed a remarkable season finale Thursday night at the Milford High School Auditorium. The superiority of this year's bands and choirs (which was recognized at Districts, according to instructors Phil Goddard, who leads the band, and Sean Nutzman, who directs the choir) brought the house to its feet twice. The second standing ovation came at the end of the program.

It was inspiring to see a medley from Lin Manuel-Miranda's *In the Heights* performed on a small stage in a simple auditorium by Nebraskans, especially when you hear them rapping quite naturally. You could tell from the students faces it had been a long winter. They had been practicing hard. It was a good winter to stay indoors. Our daughter was part of the swing choir performance. She loved the work.

The arts make young people work. The students force themselves out of their comfort zones, each and every one of them. A few had entered a new realm of comfort, at ease on the stage, mixing it up with the other performers, their conductors, and the audience. It is fun to see excellence discovered in the minds of young people, once they have seen the product of their work.

The other round of applause was for Hanano Iwatsuki. Hanano is a foreign exchange student from Japan. The band conductor, Phil Goddard, whose sense of humor was not at its usual finest, told us about Hanano.

Hanano Iwatsuki approached the band instructor last winter and told him how much she liked the band's music. He invited her to join. She played the cymbals with the rhythm section, which is a good dozen deep.

Mr. Goddard told us about Hanano teaching herself how to play the piano by watching YouTube videos over the Internet. She did not know how to read music. She taught herself using the Suzuki method.

Hanano Iwatsuki played Mozart's *Twinkle, Twinkle Little Star,* although in variations unlike those we remember from our nursery rhymes. Hanano's play was exquisite, truly remarkable. It was as though you saw glimpses of Mozart himself. Something you would pay to see.

Mr. Goddard beforehand admonished us to show Hanano a little love if she stumbled. She stumbled once, and looked at us and made the beautiful gasp of an embarrassed girl, and Hanano went right on playing Twinkle, Twinkle Little Star, her fingers rolling like waves over the ebony and ivory.

The crowd was quick to its feet. It was as though a few people in the crowd were holding it back, almost leaping to celebrate the performance of Hanano Iwatsuki, as though they could no longer contain themselves. Everyone was quick to follow.

The student from Japan stood after she had finished playing. She turned and saw us standing to greet her. She was not expecting to find us standing. It was obvious. Hanano, the dear child, was overcome. She bowed her head more in reflex than measured reaction, making it all the more authentic. She smiled, and turned away as though unsure what to do. She stood and faced us again clapped and walked off into the curtains, walking quickly, humbly stooped in posture. The crowd remained standing. We continued to clap.

Mr. Goddard appeared on the stage and was obviously surprised not to find Hanano. He hurried into the curtains and soon came out with her. He motioned her to the stage right, far in the back. Hanano bowed politely, clapped, and returned to the curtains.

The concert band, led by Mr. Goddard, closed out the evening with an encore, playing a gripping rendition of *The Battle Hymn of the Republic,* which seemed a fitting ending for a magical night. Before the band played its last number, Mr. Goddard recognized the seniors and the families he was saying goodbye to, and he asked us to once again give it up for Hanano Iwatsuki, who was standing in the back, holding her cymbals.

"That is one we'll remember," added Mr. Goddard. You could tell he meant it.

He is right.

THE MUSIC OF TUMBLEWEED LEXICON: AN ESSAY

To begin with, a few confessions: I am obsessive about music. I almost always write to music. It seems to make writing come more naturally. Sometimes, when I find myself writing without music, I am surprised I have concentrated so well so long. Often, I will replay a song for several hours while I am writing. It must be a good song that hooks me with some device or mantra, but once I find the right song to reflect the mood I am trying to achieve in a scene or action, I will replay it until either I am lost in the song or it is lost on me, or something like that. Music helps loosen my mind from everything that is around it—not only noises, but other distractions. I am now writing to Stephen Malkmus & the Jicks performing "Middle American." The song is on small playlist I made for a short story I recently completed. Earlier this evening, when I was writing something else, I listened to the Malkmus song for about an hour. I've been playing it often lately. For most of July, I listened to stuff by the Jicks, Pavement, and the Silver Jews.

On March 10, 2017, after spending a few weeks immersed in the work of Dinosaur Jr., I wrote what essentially became the first chapter (song) of a novel I have written called *Tumbleweed Lexicon*. I wrote the primary pieces of the first chapter one night as a short story about Robert Sullens and Wauneta Sullens, and how the Blizzard of 1949 separated them, and what became of the young couple after the snowstorm hit. I liked the story, and laughed at the thought that I had written a story from 1949, set in the Nebraska Sandhills, while listening to Dinosaur Jr. screaming loudly through my headphones.

The next night, I wrote a completely different story (also to Dinosaur Jr.) about an agritourism campfire ride and the characters, who became Edwin and Jackson Buck and Madeline. After a week of dabbling with both the Sullens and the Buck stories, I had the good fortune to see Dinosaur Jr. live at the Waiting Room in Omaha. I sustained the single-focused immersion through the end of the month. During that time, the idea of a novel interweaving the stories of the Sullens, the Jammers, and the Bucks started to come together in my mind.

Not long after March 31, I turned to an old favorite, Aimee Mann. On that day, the folk artist released her ninth studio album, entitled *Mental Illness,* which had early become a theme of the novel. It was then that I realized my novel was also about music. The title of my novel came from the lyrics of a song on Mann's album. I'll let you find the song yourself.

Throughout the book are scattered lyrics, usually only a word or two, from songs that kept me going, inspired me to write, and kept me company as I was writing the novel. I created a playlist of those songs. There are a few dozen songs on the playlist. Bits and pieces of lyrics, rhythms, melodies, emotions, and other intangibles from the songs are scattered throughout the manuscript. When lyrics appear in the novel, they typically denote that the song was playing during writing of that vignette, or part of it.

Music infuses the story, sets the moods, and plays during the closing scene of *Tumbleweed Lexicon.*

In early June 2017, I took our son Mac and one of his school friends to camp at Fort Robinson as a way of saying thank you for helping with the Sandhills Marathon. The day after the race, we drove west on Highway 20 as it parallels the South Dakota border. At Fort Robinson, we camped, bicycled, hiked, and adventured.

FLOATING BODIES AND RATTLESNAKES: AN ESSAY ON CAMPING AND HIKING AT FORT ROBINSON

When Soldier Creek and the White River were both running full, their waters crept from humble banks and sometimes flooded the army cemetery at Fort Robinson. Coffins and cadavers rose from the ground.

Climbing along the butte, cautious of rattlesnakes, looking down at an old army fort in a wide valley, you imagine yourself a Lakota, sizing up the scene. You had heard they were building a fort, but you had not expected to see the red-brick buildings. A sign of permanence was in the offing. But they would not find you in the hills. They could not see you watching them from the edge of the white sandstone butte.

Then you are down in the valley watching pronghorn, a buck and doe, walk to within fifty yards of your place in the grasses, sitting as the winds splashed the remains of the evening. That is where I found myself by pure happenstance after an afternoon cycling through the fort grounds and up the canyon with my son Mac and his friend Ricky. My chain broke. The people who rented the bicycles to us did not know where the trails were. There is room for improvement, but there was plenty of good and plenty worth experiencing at Fort Robinson.

This is not a history of Fort Robinson. There are many good histories. In fact, a careful follower of history would have challenged my opening paragraph. The stately red-brick officers' quarters were not built until near the end of the war with the Sioux. It was a war of attrition. Crazy Horse, the fierce Lakota warrior shaman, was killed at the fort when it was still called Camp Robinson.

After setting up our tents within a dozen paces of the cemetery, I let the boys hang out, or *chill,* as they call it (although it's something different this year), while I scouted a route for us up the butte north of the fort. We planned on hiking, climbing the next day. I did not want to waste time looking for the trailhead the morning of our hike, but the trailhead was easy to find. I parked my Highlander and walked up the trail a little. We would have no trouble finding it. It would take us five minutes from our camp to reach it. I knew everything I needed to know. I would leave exploring to the boys the next day. I headed back toward camp.

As I was driving back to the campsite, I spotted the two pronghorn near a water tank, filled by an old metal windmill. Welcoming the interruption, and supposing the boys would not notice my extended absence, I stopped my vehicle, got out, and closed the door softly. I walked a good quarter mile down a light trail, then sat in the grass and watched the pronghorn. They began walking away from the water tank and windmill. They walked toward the setting sun, back up the main canyon. I would watch them walk away. It would be a wonderful way to watch the sunset.

Then, the pronghorn surprised me and circled up the slope to the north, toward me. The buck and the doe bent their path toward me. Many call pronghorn antelope, but they are not antelope. They are not related to the antelope in Africa, although their Latin name—*Antilocapra americana*—might suggest they are. The pronghorn seems the fleetest of animals native to the Great Plains. They are brilliantly painted, each a unique combination of the grassy amber of the autumn hillsides and white. The buck's short horns are sculpted into two prongs: one protruding forward, and another, more delicate piece curling back.

I knew they saw me. They would walk a few steps, look at me, eat some grass, and repeat all the things I watched them do in no order. They approached me to within fifty yards. I began to wonder if they would come eat out of my hands.

The male turned to the west and trotted away. The doe was slow to follow. I believed she fancied me (see notes).

Without question, the curiosity of the antelope fascinates me.

Back at the campsite, hiking toward the half-light of the sun on the higher slopes beyond our tents, the boys wanted to walk through the cemetery. I told them they had to read the historical marker first. It told us the cemetery flooded frequently because of its location at the confluence of Soldier Creek and the White River. I told the boys coffins floated out of their graves. The boys read and no longer wanted to walk through the cemetery. The echoes of ghosts stir the conscious and gives death new meaning.

The wonderful thing about Nebraska's historical markers is that they keep you honest. I had convinced my memory that the sign had told us floodwaters forced coffins from the ground. In tracking down the sign, I found no such fact mentioned. There was nothing to suggest it, either. See for yourself. I laughed and had to account for the story honestly. But it seemed a good twist, plausible, and it got the boys' attention. There's a small spadeful of history they will likely remember.

We continued to the White River, meager and clean and tumbling over some concrete contraption that needed a few sticks of dynamite. I took my shoes off before I crossed the creek. It was six inches deep at the center. The boys did the same.

On the other side of the river, I dried off my feet and put back on my socks and hiking shoes. The boys ran on barefoot.

"You better put your shoes on," I told them.

"Why?" my son asked, with a tone of friendly defiance in his twelve-year-old voice. His friend joined him in posture.

"Rattlesnakes."

The boys looked at me, quizzically.

I went on. "I'll see the big ones, or they'll see me, and slither off. The little ones," I said. "It's the little ones you can't see. They might strike, but they can't bite through my shoe."

I laughed as the boys looked down at their feet. They sat down and put on their shoes. They walked behind me to the fence that looked over the wilderness to the south: wild land that looks the way it looked when Indians camped along the White River. The Red Cloud Agency was just downstream from our campsite. The boys stood atop a fence post and looked as the half-light drew into the sky.

On the hike back to the campsite, I asked the boys what they'd do if it rained a lot tonight.

They did not point out the cloudless sky, but only looked at me.

"What if the White River floods?" I asked.

The boys were old enough to understand the suggestion, but not old enough to find it amusing.

We returned quietly to our campsite beside the cemetery.

After we had settled in for the night, I told the boys how Crazy Horse was killed not far from where we were sleeping, back when there were no red-brick buildings. I told them how the manner of his death gave form to the vision he experienced when he was about their age. I reminded them Crazy Horse had seen the same stars, here, where we camped. We looked at the stars speckling the blackness until falling asleep.

Every clear night in northwestern Nebraska is a wonder of light.

In the morning, I boiled water over a small gas stove, and we ate a simple breakfast of oatmeal, hot chocolate, and coffee. We drove to the trailhead, passing a horse-drawn wagon that was carrying a few tourists. We reached the trailhead and found a few men preparing breakfast over a fire for the approaching wagonful. The food smelled good, but the oatmeal had filled us. We said hello to the chefs as we walked from our vehicle to the trailhead.

Ricky, Mac, and I hiked up the slope from the trailhead to the top of the ridgeline, running east and west with the precision of a compass. Majestic, sandstone white buttes project like columns along the ridgeline. The ridge of proud buttes stands as a stately backdrop to the red brick buildings of the fort. I prompted our assault on the edge of one white butte. We reached the promontory and looked out like Sioux at the fort below us. Closer, from the base of the cliff, almost directly below us, wafted the endearing smell of bacon and smoke from the cook fire. Sitting at picnic tables like ducks were the tourists.

Unarmed and less dangerous, we explored other buttes and slowly crawled down some small canyon, finding our way toward the trailhead. There is always a path, even if you cannot see it. Sometimes you find your own way down.

We crawled down a small series of ledges, checking each step and handhold for rattlesnakes, and found ourselves walking into the picnic area itself. The boys walked proudly, knowing the fear they overcame. I walked through the cook site with a sense of amusement. My only regret is that we had not thought of war paint. The group of tourists had to be surprised by a rough-looking threesome (we'd spent the night in tents) walking down from the buttes, the trees, and all of rattlesnake territory, through their picnic area and back to our vehicle.

In life, there is usually a catch, and sometimes that catch makes life better.

Among the tourists were two friends of mine who happen not to be tourists, but experts in the outdoors. Knowing I sometimes stray from the beaten path, my friends were perhaps less surprised to see me and the boys than the rest of the group.

I told them what we had been doing. I bragged up the boys and told my friends, perhaps a little loudly, that we had not seen any rattlesnakes.

After we left, one of the tourists asked my friends whether I had been serious about the rattlesnakes.

My friend responded that he believed I had been serious. During an entire day of touring the fort grounds, the ridge, and the canyons, the tourists would not step out of the jeep unless they were on concrete or asphalt.

Mac, Ricky, and I returned to our camp, struck our tents, warm and dried in the mid-morning Panhandle. We packed and headed southwest to visit the Agate Fossil Beds.

Summer hiking in rattlesnake country: *honestly, it's not for everyone.*

This is a fictionalized account of the 1873 massacre of an estimated 80 Pawnee men, women, and children. No one bothered to get an accurate body count. Their killers were two tribes of Lakota. The United States government dispatched an agent to look over each tribe. All three agents had some complicity in the massacre. The story is told through the eyes of the agents, who meet up in an Ogallala saloon a few years later.

BURNING BREEZES: THE STORY OF MASSACRE CANYON

I was tending bar when I saw them walk through the swinging doors of the Crystal Palace. The Frenchman, Janis, entered first. His beard was not neatly trimmed like when I'd seen him before, and he looked tired, but he seemed at ease, like he was thinking a little live music would do him some good. He was looking at the stage, and you could tell he was listening as Benny played the piano. Antoine Janis then looked toward the bar and saw me. He nodded in recognition. The agent named Stephen Estes walked behind Janis. Estes was nondescript: Dirty brown hair. The height of any other man who might walk into the saloon. He did not sulk, but he did not walk like a soldier. Estes looked at me, and it seemed he was in little mood to renew our acquaintance.

* * * * *

I had been an agent for the Pawnee. I rode on their last buffalo hunt into the valley of the Republican River during the summer of 1873. Not long after, I retired from government life and moved to Ogallala. I had settled down and built a home in the town some called *the Gomorrah of the plains* at the terminus of the Texas Road. My girl would be dancing on the stage later that evening in her short, silky purple skirt that matched the very little she wore on top and the garter around her fishnet hose. Her name was *Mariah*. Most other uses of the name have been false. Her name was Mariah, and I only felt it after she had passed. Her name remains branded across my heart. Mariah kicked higher than any of the other girls, and her smile was the sweetest. I sometimes wonder if my comparisons affected my judgment.

   Janis and Estes had been agents for two tribes of Sioux. Janis was an agent for the Oglala. Estes was an agent for the Brulé.

We had all been trail agents dispatched under orders of the United States Army to chaperone a tribe that had spent centuries crossing the parched grasslands and burning breezes, migrating with the seasons, following the buffalo, and hunting.

The days of Indians crossing the plains had now ended. Cattle were being driven, dry-tongued and mad, from river upon river, climbing the ladder from Texas. Janis and Estes were on a drive that had just arrived from Tascosa.

I knew a little about each of them—had met Estes two more times than I cared to remember, and had been introduced to Janis. What we all had in common was a massacre. Each of us were all involved in it in different ways. I believed each of us equally responsible, but for some reason, I always held Estes to a deeper account.

I had picked up wind that the two had become friends and rode cattle drives together. Janis was well regarded as a hard-working hand. I heard other hands say that he was prone to working like he was possessed by something. He was not afraid to run off a bandit or to trail a stray into a long canyon. He seemed oblivious to the risks. No one said much about Estes, except that he was quiet. I figured it was on account of him never coming to terms with the fact that he did not have the same blood on his hands as Janis and me. The first time I met the man, he had little to say to me. I never cared for him.

* * * * *

Both men walked up to the bar and extended a hand to me before they sat down. It was early evening. There was room at the bar even after the two men sat down. Janis ordered a beer, and I told him I was surprised to find a Frenchmen not ordering a bottle of wine. He laughed. He wore a thick beard and moustache and had a grin I did not remember from the time we met one another, a couple of years after the incident that brought our trails together.

Estes ordered a beer, too.

We talked a little. I heard about the drive they had just finished. Janis told me he had bought a little land around a spring called the Birdwood northeast of Ogallala. He was going to start a ranch, and he was looking for a pretty little gal to settle down with.

Estes just shook his head.

* * * * *

We talked about many things, but Janis kept returning to our common history. Eventually, our pasts catch up with us. We revisit them in mind and spirit. Sometimes our journeys back bring us answers. Janis wanted to talk about the massacre. I suspected there was something about it that he wanted to get off his chest.

I had found myself that way from time to time. I still do, but I refrain from bringing it up with others. Even with the friends I have told, I don't want them thinking I dwell on the incident. But I do dwell on it. It haunts my thoughts each day. One hundred and fifty Pawnee dead. The eyes of the living and the dead, of men, women, and children. The eyes—the eyes and a weakness of grip. All the things I might have done differently. I suspected Janis wanted to clear his mind. I was glad to oblige and, perhaps in turn, clear mine.

* * * * *

I did not figure Estes would have much to say, and he did not. Janis had many things to tell us. We talked for a while. Occasionally, Janis brought up something about the massacre, but we had not talked about it long. We chattered about meaningless things as I was pouring drinks for other men at the bar and the cocktail waitresses, whose pace was picking up as the evening outside darkened.

"How did you wind up with the Pawnee?" Janis asked me at one point.

I smiled. It was a good question, and one I was not asked every day. I answered him with a story that sounded something like this:

* * * * *

I never intended to be a trail agent for the Pawnee. I began my work at the fort near the Pawnee reservation after spending a couple years failing as a Nebraska corn farmer up north in Boone County. I could go on and on about how I was better with horses than crops and how I wound up as a barn hand at the fort near Genoa. I'd worked at the fort for a few months, but I was not a soldier. I took care of the officers' horses and helped with the rest of the herd. I'd been taking care of horses since I could carry a bucket full of the manure my father picked from his horse's stall.

The officers liked the work I did. I enjoyed working with the horses and was good at making the officers laugh. One of the senior officers told me I needed to get out and see Indian country before it was completely gone so I would have some real stories to tell.

Two days before Independence Day, Sergeant Rodysill handed me a letter. We had been planning a large celebration at the fort. Cannons would be fired, and light artillery. The letter was from General Allen. He had appointed me trail agent for the Pawnee, who were heading to the Republican River valley on their annual buffalo hunt. The general directed me to accompany them and charged me with a number of responsibilities. I was to watch over the Pawnee's small remnant—no more than four hundred men, women, and children—and make sure they did not bother any of the settlers or have trouble with other tribes. The general's letter also appointed a kid named Lester Beach Platt to ride along and help me. It had been a few years since the Pawnee caused any trouble.

I accepted the charge after they agreed to let me take the auburn mare I had grown fond of. Most of the horses were high-strung, especially the officers' horses—on account of lack of exercise, I believed. The mare was not lazy, but was of a pleasant demeanor. She liked to nuzzle me with the soft muzzle of her nose. I fed her from my hand. I called the mare Rosa.

They dispatched me the next morning onto the trail with the Pawnee. There was no visible trail. The Pawnee followed something they could see that I could not. We rode our horses into the hills southwest of the small reservation. By mid-morning, the sun shimmered white in the sky. False waters of mirages rose up before us.

One night, only a few days into the pilgrimage, Ute raiders came in the darkness and stole a few of our horses. I talked with one of my

Pawnee friends about it that night by the fire. There was some dancing and talk of war.

I had learned to communicate with a young hunter named White Arrow through a combination of gestures and speech. He picked up English remarkably well while we were together. He was friendly with me. We would joke with one another. He had a harder time saying my name than any other English I taught him. There was, of course, no trouble with *John*. *John* came naturally to him, like the name of a brother. Rather, it was somewhere near the middle of *Williamson* that things broke down.

White Arrow also told me serious things. White Arrow told me the ghost of his father was an eagle and could see the Utes riding away to the west. The eagle, with its white head and sharp eyes, saw beyond the dust of the Utes toward the desolation of what is now northeastern Colorado and saw large camps of Sioux.

"How do they sneak up on them without the horses making any noises?" I asked White Arrow about the Utes' raid.

"The Utes are good. The Sioux are better," he replied.

"How's that?" I asked.

"The horses think they are us."

"How do you know that?"

"The Sioux send men who speak our language, and they talk to the horses," the young man said. "They whisper. The Sioux are fine horse thieves."

"How do you know the Sioux speak your language?" I asked White Arrow. "Have you heard them?"

"When I was a boy, I was watching the horses one night. I could hear whispering from the hill across the grasses where we were keeping our horses. I listened as the men approached. I heard them talking to the horses. They talked with one another in the Pawnee language."

"How did you know they were Sioux?" I somehow thought to ask, adding, "It was dark."

"The next morning, I found a war axe one of them dropped when they ran away. They did not stay long after I fired my rifle at them. My father was very proud. It was an Oglala war axe. There was no disagreement about it. One of the men said he believed it the old war axe of Crazy Horse. I cannot say that is true. The old men and my father let me keep it."

White Arrow showed the war axe to me.

* * * * *

"What did it look like?" asked Estes. I had almost forgotten he was there. I had been talking to Janis.

"Did the Pawnee pursue the Ute thieves?" asked Janis.

"They elected not to," I responded.

"The Utes," Janis began, then stopped for a moment. "It must have been the Utes who stole horses from the Oglala camp, too."

Estes said, "We were camped on the other side of the South Platte, about one night south of here. I was with more than a thousand Oglala. I remember hearing that some horses were stolen from the tribe. Utes were suspected. A few Oglala men pursued, but didn't catch the thieves."

Janis went on. "We moved into Nebraska and spent a night on the high plains between the Platte and the Republican, and then we rode into the valley of the Frenchman River, where we encamped. That night at the fires, the Oglala talked of revenge."

* * * * *

Estes camped to the northwest, not far from Julesburg, with a tribe of nearly 750 Brulé Sioux, who were waiting for rations to arrive. The same night the Utes rode off with Oglala horses, the call of the buffalo grew stronger than the faith of the Brul in the coming rations. They decided to move on. The next morning, the Brul filed out toward their old hunting grounds, where they had frequently encountered the Pawnee.

By some strange twist of fate, the Brul came upon their Oglala cousins in the Frenchman valley. The tribes joined and made an immense camp that lit low clouds in the night sky. Both Janis and Estes said it was mere happenstance. They had heard not one word of speculation that the other tribe might be in the Republican basin, let alone the Frenchman Valley. The Sioux chalked up the reunion to the spirits of their fathers. Recalling their passion for revenge, driven by the horse thieves from the previous night, the Oglala saw it as a sign of a great victory.

The spirits did not tell them, then, over whom the victory would be. The Sioux chanted and made a war dance before the fires. They danced long into the night, their music becoming one with the stars, sparkling through the darkness.

* * * * *

On most of the days of the buffalo hunt, the Pawnee moved. We walked and rode, and the children played or slouched miserably as fatigue caught up with their spirits. Seldom did we camp long at one place. We were moving the horses, finding fresh grass for them, and looking for buffalo. When we camped longer, we scouted other places and scoured the canyonland, looking for buffalo.

White Arrow told me stories his father and the older men had told him about their tangles with the Sioux. He told me his grandfather told him that when he was a boy, the Sioux and the Pawnee were enemies, and they had fought over land since he was a young man, when they started getting horses from the Comanche in the warmer lands. The Sioux were quick to fight, and when they had horses, it was easier to fight other tribes; the more horses they had, the less they took things out on their brothers and cousins.

White Arrow told me the Sioux are fearless in attack. No man becomes a warrior unless he is willing to lay his fears behind him and run into a battle as though he was running into darkness, unsure what he was stepping into.

"Sounds like they are crazy," I observed, when he was first telling me about the Sioux.

"They are not crazy. They would not let their crazy men fight," said White Arrow. "The Sioux are brave, and they are cruel. They have not been good to our women. We taught our boys to kill themselves rather than be taken."

"What did they do to the women and boys?"

"I will tell you later, when there are not children around."

I had forgotten we were sitting in White Arrow's tipi. He and I sat near the opening. His wife and children had fallen asleep.

* * * * *

One day in mid-July, I had wandered up a ravine with Lester Platt, White Arrow, and a couple other young Pawnee men. They had been sent to scout for buffalo, and White Arrow asked us to go with them. Platt was walking in the bottom of the ravine. Occasionally, on hot days, an old bull would bed down in the murky water in the lowland shadowed by the cottonwood: an easy target, unable to fight or run—a good week of food. Platt shouted, calling the rest of us to the canyon floor.

"Buffalo," Platt said, pointing to a bare skeleton, nearly complete and intact.

White Arrow shook his head. He was standing on the other side of the ravine. "Mountain lion," he said.

I shook my head. I thought White Arrow was joking with me again.

He cracked a smile and motioned me to come over to his side of the ravine. Beneath the buffalo, visible from the other side of the ravine, was the white skeleton of a mountain lion, also entirely intact. The giant cat's skull had been crushed, as though by the point of a spear.

I pointed to the bison's horn.

White Arrow nodded.

We camped away from the tribe that night. The five of us lay under blankets, looking at the stars, talking a little, trying to fall asleep.

"You see that one," I said to the Pawnee men, pointing to the southern sky. "Sagittarius," I said. "That's what we call it."

One of the men said the word *Sagittarius*, or tried a couple times.

"Archer. He is the archer," I told them. Then, I pointed again, drawing the figure of the constellation, the shapes of the man's upper body, his bow, and the readied arrow, in the sky.

The Pawnee watched the pattern my finger traced, and then looked at the sky until they found the form. It did not take long. I drew it only a few times. They nodded, and traced the constellation of stars themselves.

I then told them that Sagittarius was a centaur, part man—I pointed to my upper body—and part horse. I pointed to my legs.

The men laughed at me. "Horse?" White Arrow said, smiling, shaking his head at me. He made me laugh. It was good to laugh at myself, I found.

"Part horse, part man," I said, standing my ground. I pointed at my upper body and then again at my legs. In the darkness of the earth, I don't think the other men could see.

White Arrow asked, "What about the middle?"

We all laughed.

White Arrow was a good man, with a pretty wife and a couple of kids. One of his children, a young boy who acted very mature, was learning English from me. He helped me with my Pawnee and Spanish.

"Sagittarius," White Arrow said all wrong. We laughed at him.

"The archer," I said.

He nodded. "The archer," he said earnestly. "My grandfather, watching me."

I knew nothing would answer him more clearly than a nod, so I nodded.

White Arrow went on, "With my father, the eagle."

* * * * *

Before we left one another for our separate sleep journeys, White Arrow told me the bones of the mountain lion and buffalo were a bad omen. I laughed, but he stared at me as though his face was turning to stone. In that moment, his face looked very old—cold, sober, and old. He had seen something I could not. We stared at one another until I shut my eyes and fell into sleep.

We woke in the morning. The sky was clear and starting to whiten as it does in the canyonland of southwest Nebraska, in the upper reaches of the Republican basin. We rode to the nearest hilltop. From there, we could see no buffalo. White Arrow turned his horse and kicked it vigorously—almost wildly—into a full gallop.

When we returned to the main camp, I asked White Arrow why he had ridden away so quickly.

"There were no buffalo."

"We could've gone further, looking."

He shook his head.

"Why not?"

"I am no fool. The Sioux are in these hills. They would prey on a small band of us. It would be worse for the boy," said White Arrow, nodding toward Platt.

* * * * *

The hunt moved along. We killed a few buffalo every week. From my vantage point on the muscular back of my red mare, Rosa, the journey was less about the bounty than devotion to a ritual that had purified Pawnee spirits over many epochs. Men hunted. Women prepared meals, assembled their tipis and struck them, and seemed constantly in motion. The children helped their mothers and played games—some of them organized, others pure frolic. Dogs played with the children and sometimes fought one another. I found the nomadic life pleasing, leaving the cares of each night in an old camp.

One late afternoon, while I was helping White Arrow's wife set up *the kitchen*—as the women were now calling it to play along with me—three white men walked into our camp. We had been working our way back down the Republican valley and had heard growing rumors about the Sioux. Spirits continued to warn White Arrow, but the older men had grown weary of his admonitions. Nothing had come of them.

One of the white men, a young man with dirty, unkempt hair, a thick beard, and a dark, sun-dried face that made him look older than he was, approached me. He was a miscreant, I am certain, but I could see in his eyes that he was sincere. He had wandered by our camp from the north with two other rough-looking men.

The young man walked directly to me and looked me in the eyes and told me "the entire damn Sioux nation" was "camping in some canyon twenty-five miles to the northwest." He said they were "looking for trouble." I never knew if he meant the Sioux or the Pawnee.

I took the young miscreant to Sky Chief, who looked the young man up and down with contempt, but listened to what he had to say. After hearing him, Sky Chief called the man a liar.

"The white men try to scare the Pawnee away from our hunting grounds so they can kill our buffalo," said Sky Chief with little expression.

The man walked away after calling the chief a "dumb fucking old Ponca."

Sky Chief asked me to translate what the man had said, although I knew he spoke enough English to understand the point being made.

In Pawnee, I told Sky Chief the man had called him "a dumb fucking old Indian."

"Did he call me a *Ponca?*" asked Sky Chief in the clearest English.

I did not know how to take the old man and merely looked at him.

The old man started laughing and took me by the shoulder.

I laughed a little with him, but his laugh did not seem genuine.

"I am a *Ponca*," said Sky Chief, holding me awkwardly, laughing again. I do not know that the Pawnee actually held the Ponca Indians in low esteem, but Sky Chief certainly made it sound that way. With the same exaggerated tone of disgust, he repeated himself. "I am a *Ponca*, and you—you are a coward and a squaw."

Sky Chief, the old man who was wiry but muscular, pushed his body from mine aggressively. I walked back two steps and looked at him.

"I will go as far as you dare go," I said, holding the man's eyes in mine. "Don't forget that."

Sky Chief nodded, looking me sternly in the eyes.

* * * * *

I stopped talking and took a drink of the sarsaparilla I had concocted with local ingredients. After a few weeks of experimentation, I had developed a flavor I liked. The owner of the place liked it, too. He gave me permission to sell it at the saloon in return for a cut of my profits.

"Now—now, let me tell you my story, Williamson," broke in Janis before I had a chance to swallow. I finished and laughed at the young Frenchman. Even Estes seemed mildly amused. It was the first time I had seen the man smile. Janis went on, and we listened.

"This is what happened," Janis said soberly, putting the interjection of lightness behind us.

"The old chief, Little Wound, told me that several scouts had come upon a large Pawnee camp. He told me about the history of animus between the Sioux and the Pawnee. The old man reminded me I had advised them against going into Ute territory to settle the score of the horses, and he told me "the Pawnees are better horse thieves than the Utes," and he did not want to lose horses again.

"I admit to being softened by the old man's witty *non-sequitur,* but he did not bat at an eye me. He glared at me, as though he was searching me for an answer."

Janis stopped and smiled at me. In the instant of his expression, I found myself chuckling at Janis. Estes was not smiling. He was looking intently at Janis.

"Go on," Estes said, sounding somewhat bothered. "What did you say to the chief?"

Janis looked at Estes, and nodded. "I told the old chief this. I can recite my words. They are written in my conscience."

"Well, what were they?" asked Estes, which started me laughing.

Janis smiled, cocked his head a little, and went on.

"The chief looked at me. He spoke again before I responded. He asked me whether I had 'received any orders not to allow them to fight the Pawnee.' I thought on it."

Janis looked me in the eyes and went on, "I had orders not to allow the Oglala to go to the Pawnee reservation or to fight with the whites,

93

but I had no orders prohibiting fighting with the Pawnee in the Republican basin." Janis stopped for a moment, took a last long sip of his beer, and repeated, "I had *no orders prohibiting fighting the Pawnee someplace off the reservation.*"

After a moment, I asked Janis if he would like another drink, and he told me he would. I looked at Estes. He nodded at me. He did not smile, but I could feel a connection in our exchange of looks. After I had poured a glass of beer for each man, Estes surprised me by speaking. I think he surprised Janis, too.

"After two nights together with the Oglala—Janis knows this," said Estes. "We—the Brulé—broke camp and moved north. We had not gone far. We were camping just past the river they call the Stinking Water. A couple Oglala galloped into our camp and spoke to the older men of the tribe. I listened. I could pick up some of what they were saying, something about *the Pawnee.* There was talk of battle. Later, one of the Brulé warriors told me the Oglala said they found Pawnee in the area. The Oglala had said the Pawnee were probably the horse thieves and not the Utes. The Oglala asked the Brulé to join in an attack on the Pawnee.

"The men told me that the Brulé have the right to make war on the Pawnee. When I asked them how that was, one of the older men said that Janis told this to the Oglala.

"'Janis said they have the right to attack the Pawnee?' I asked him.

"'Janis told the Oglala this,' the old man told me.

"'Well, then the Oglala can go make war on the Pawnee,' I said to him.

"The chief told me it was their right by nature or something," said Estes. "They said they had as good a right to make war upon the Pawnee as the Oglala. How was I to argue? No one ever explained all them treaties to me."

Janis chuckled. Estes smiled with him.

"I explained to the old fella that it was not me that told them they had the right to make war on the Pawnee," said Estes.

"Then the old chief smiled at me," Estes said. "And the old man said, 'We will not make war on the Pawnee. We will only ride with our brothers, the Oglala.'"

Estes took a drink. A few moments followed, and no one spoke. The sounds of the saloon filled the silence—Benny on the piano, the girls now singing, glasses knocking wooden tabletops, chattering, laughter—nothing you followed long.

Janis spoke again, but his tone was different. He spoke as though he were someplace else. "It was the best thing that could happen. Let them live, kill. It was their last massacre. They were bound to have one last massacre, and they had it. My only sadness is that it was their last, but you can't never bottle the past."

* * * * *

I often wondered why I had held Estes in disdain until that moment. Estes was no different. I had failed to assert myself because my manhood had been called into question. Janis had given thoughtlessly strict construction to his orders. Estes merely acquiesced to Janis's false acquiescence. He had been no more complicit than Janis or I—perhaps less.

"That evening," I said, stepping back into the conversation tentatively. I looked at the men. Estes was still looking into the bottom of his glass. Janis was looking behind me, into the mirror behind the bar or somewhere. I went on. I don't remember exactly how I put it.

* * * * *

The council took the ordinary precautions that evening after the young miscreant had warned us about the Sioux. A group of older boys was summoned to watch the horses. No sentries were stationed elsewhere on the perimeters. No scouts were dispatched. No thoughts of what may be coming from the northwest were voiced.

Shadows stretched long from the cottonwoods, and the inescapable heat of the day at last started to wane. Everyone wanted to leave the heat behind, but I worried what might come in the night. Others saw a pleasant evening early in the month of the August, with flowers in full bloom and the western meadowlark warbling goodnight. The Pawnee settled down to sleep as their fires crackled to cinders.

I did not try to stay awake. I was not on guard, but I could not fall asleep. I shut my eyes, but could not sleep. I did nothing but listen to the noises of the night. The soft breathing of the Pawnee, the hum of the chorus of crickets, the occasional bullfrog down the canyon, closer to the comfort of the river. My thoughts wandered back to my parents on the dairy in Wisconsin, to the fort and the barn and the horses. My mare was with the other horses, hobbled not far outside camp. My thoughts wandered and stumbled upon my duties to the tribe, and for some reason, I wondered why I had not thought to order the chief to send out scouts. It was squarely within my power.

By the time I thought of sending scouts, it was too late. The chief was sleeping. I was afraid to wake him.

Under their blankets, the Pawnee people slept. I found myself falling into the rhythm of their breathing. The sound rose from the blackness of the ground. It led me to thoughts of the day. Only a couple of the old Pawnee women had been in the *kitchen* and heard the young white man's warning. They were not about to give his words honor by telling others. None of the people were awake worrying about the Sioux. They knew nothing to stir worry in them. They did not know the Sioux were near.

I looked into the sky and saw Sagittarius. I thought of my good friend White Arrow and his father and his grandfather. I felt eyes looking down at me, not stars.

* * * * *

In the morning, Sky Chief apologized to me for what he had said.

I asked him if we should send scouts out ahead.

He shook his head but smiled at me.

I thought for a moment about my power, but Sky Chief had taken the high road, and I did not want to spoil the conversation.

He told me we were going up the canyon from the Republican. We would climb to the table on the top and then descend to the Frenchman River in a day or two.

We made our way up the canyon. I can still see the women and children walking. Only a few old people were on a travois. Older men and women had stayed on the reservation. Dogs trotted in and out of the procession. Boys rode ponies aimlessly. The young men were in front, the sides, and the rear, but they were under no heightened watch.

A few young men had ridden up to the east ridge and came back to the group, reporting buffalo on the table ahead. Sky Chief told me he was going to look. He rode off. Later I learned he was the first one shot. He had killed a buffalo and was skinning it when the Sioux came upon him. He was struck during the first volley and died fighting.

The Sioux poured into the canyon like a flood. Pawnee men, the old and the young, the strong and the meager, rode up to meet them. Women and children and the pack horses were ordered down the canyon. Dogs dashed *helter skelter.* Some were chasing the Sioux. They recognized an enemy. Others ran before the women and children, as though leading the way toward safety. Sioux warriors, perched on both west and east ridges above the canyon, were firing down on the Pawnee as they fled.

I spoke hastily with one of the elders, who was standing near me in battle. I trusted his judgment. We agreed the men should fall back, down the canyon, protecting the women and children. We could mount our defense in the trees. The elder told the others, but one man, Fighting Bear, shouted we should make our stand where we stood. He gestured at the ground. After ordering Platt down the canyon with the women and children, I remained and fought.

The Sioux swarmed around us. I fired as quickly as I could, waiting for an arrow or bullet, a moment of pain, hoping I would be killed before they reached me. One of the older men asked if I might ride out and parlay with the Sioux, to see if something could be worked out. The old man motioned with his hand toward White Arrow. "He will interpret for you."

I could not tell him no. I was no coward. The old Pawnee handed me a staff with white feathers tied around the spearhead. White Arrow and I trotted out, as calmly as we could, toward the Sioux. One of them shot the white flag out of my hand. I saw White Arrow turn his horse at the same time my auburn mare turned on her own. We retreated toward the cottonwoods, racing beside one another. I lost sight of White Arrow as I rode past the front line. I had almost made it to a thicket of cottonwoods and into the relative safety of the women and children when the Sioux shot my horse, Rosa, out from underneath me. I clambered to my feet, ignoring for a moment the cactus in my palm, and scrambled into the trees. Behind a large cottonwood, I fired my pistol at painted Sioux warriors as they rode by, chasing the Pawnee.

White Arrow lay on the ground ten steps from me. Horses trampled his body.

As I was firing, White Arrow's son ran up to me with his father's horse. He pointed back to his mother, who was holding his younger brother. She nodded and looked at the horse. I mounted, and the boy tied a strip of red flannel on the horse's bridle and slapped its flanks with a sharp, loud cry. He ran back toward his mother. I rode off and provided cover as the women and children fled down the canyon.

When I could see no more of the living in the canyon above me, I turned the horse and rode away.

* * * * *

The Sioux were not reckless or wild. They were methodical. They killed and took their scalps and showed no thought of looting or theft. They had come merely to kill. Suddenly, they turned and rode away.

One time, I had a dream that the US cavalry rode in and chased away the Sioux as they attacked us. But the Sioux had simply turned around as though they had gotten their fill of revenge. I have many dreams about the battle. I remember the eyes of the living and the dead. The eyes I remember most clearly, like terrible stars, are the eyes of a little Pawnee girl I rode by. The Sioux were chasing me on White Arrow's horse. I reached for the girl, leaning and reaching as far as I could without falling, and I wanted to grab her and take her away. I was able to grasp the girl's hand for an instant, but then mine was pulled away by the speed of the horse. My grip was not strong enough to hold her. I could not turn back or—I only remember I saw her eyes. I still see her eyes.

Before I left the reservation, White Arrow's widow and son visited me. The boy handed me a feather. He told me in the broken English I had been teaching him that the feather would remind me of an arrow. It came from an eagle. Now his father could see from the sky like the eagle. He knew his father would watch over me.

* * * * *

At last, I had made my confession. The men finished their drinks. The night had grown long. The girls on the stage and Mariah took their first break.

I poured the men a drink. "Last one?" I asked.

Both nodded and tipped their glasses toward me.

"What you say that constellation was, the one you told Yellow Arrow about?" asked Estes, the quiet one.

"White Arrow?"

"What constellation did you tell White Arrow about?"

"Sagittarius."

"Yeah. Sagittarius. The archer. That's right."

I smiled at Estes. Janis slapped him on the back, like a brother would.

RESOURCES AND FURTHER READING

The following works either informed or inspired me. Some are books I referenced—histories, for example. Some are mentioned to suggest further reading on things that might interest you.

Snowbound: A Story of the Blizzard of 1949

- *Blizzard of 1949,* Roy V. Alleman (1991)
- *The Valentine Republican* (weekly editions between November 1948 and March 1949)
- *The Blizzard of '49,* WyomingPBS (2015)
- *Winter of 1948–1949,* Alan J. Bartels, *Nebraska Life* (January 2019)

Juanita Sullens: An Essay on the Art of Changing Faces

- *Crazy Horse: Strange Man of the Oglalas,* Mari Sandoz. 1942. University of Nebraska Press, 1963.
- Several other biographies and other works also have helped shape my images of Crazy Horse. Sandoz's work is the most colorful, but it pales against other of her treasures like *Old Jules* and *The Horsecatcher.*
- *Blue Water Creek and the First Sioux War,* 1854–1856, R. Eli Paul. University of Oklahoma Press, 2004.
- *The First Sioux War, the Grattan Fight and Blue Water Creek,* 1854–1856, Paul N. Beck. University Press of America, 2004.
- *Sandhills Hidden Water,* featuring Blue Water Creek, NET (2011).

Widower: A Poem about Goose Hunting in Garden County

- *Widower* was originally published in the wonderful state journal of culture and life, *Nebraska Life* (November/December 2004). Dedicated to Dr. Malone.

MHS Fine Arts Puts on Remarkable Season Finale: The Story of Hanano Iwatsuki

- Originally published in *The Milford Times* (May 15, 2019), our fine local newspaper.

Floating Bodies and Rattlesnakes: An Essay on Camping and Hiking at Fort Robinson

- "Honestly, it's not for everyone" is a slogan developed to help Nebraska promote itself as a tourism destination, the ingenious product of the Nebraska Travel Commission. The slogan, I think, is spot on in its wit and honesty—quintessential Nebraska.

Burning Breezes: The Story of Massacre Canyon

- The historical background comes mainly from "The Battle of Massacre Canyon," Paul D. Riley, *The Nebraska Indian Wars Reader: 1865–1877,* ed. R. Eli Paul. University of Nebraska Press, 1998.

MASSACRE CANYON PLAYLIST

The essay in this Anthology on the music of *Tumbleweed Lexicon* will tell you more about music's influence on my writing. I will add here only that when I write about a subject that very much intrigues me, such as the battle of Massacre Canyon, I find music that helps give me a sense of the mood of scenes I am trying to imagine. Music greases my skids. It helps me break loose from other worries and fancies to reach for some deeper essence. Music lifts me up and helps me see from a different horizon. The following songs helped inspire the spirit of the story:

- "Gold Soundz," Pavement, *Crooked Rain*
- "Forgotten Graves," The Brian Jonestown Massacre, *Forgotten Graves*
- "Feel the Pain," Dinosaur Jr., *Without a Sound*
- "Bad," A Ferocious Jungle Cat, *Nebraskan Thunderfunk*
- "Strange," Galaxie 500, *On Fire*
- "Silence Kid," Pavement, *Crooked Rain*
- "Stop Breathin," Pavement, *Crooked Rain*
- "Heaven is a Truck (Egg Shell)," Pavement, *Crooked Rain*
- "Grounded," Pavement, *Crooked Rain*
- "Smith & Jones Forever," Silver Jews, *American Water*
- "Cast Off," Stephen Malkmus & The Jicks, *Sparkle Hard*
- "Shiggy," Stephen Malkmus & The Jicks, *Sparkle Hard*
- "Like a Fool," Superchunk, *Foolish*
- "Pale Blue Eyes," The Velvet Underground, *The Velvet Underground*
- "From a Motel 6," Yo La Tengo, *Painful*
- "Middle America," Stephen Malkmus & The Jicks, *Sparkle Hard*

ABOUT THE AUTHOR

Andrew Pollock recently completed a novel titled *Tumbleweed Lexicon,* set in the vast Nebraska backcountry called the Sandhills. Andrew grew up in on the southern reaches of the Sandhills in rural Keith County, the son of local newspaper publishers. He and his wife live with their kids and dozen or so animals in rural Seward County, outside the village of Pleasant Dale. During the day, Andy practices law in Lincoln. Andrew's spirit resides in Cherry County, the heart of the Nebraska Sandhills, where he fly-fishes, golfs, hikes, camps, watches stars, and coordinates an annual marathon he and friends started in 2007. The race has attracted runners from all over the United States and two other countries who come to run on a one-lane blacktop road forty miles from Valentine. Bovine spectators far outnumber humans.